The
LOVE AN

JOURNAL

Jim Fay & Foster W. Cline, M.D.

TENTH ANNIVERSARY
COLLECTION

The Love and Logic®
PRESSInc.
Golden, Colorado
www.loveandlogic.com

www.loveandlogic.com

Illustrations by Paule Botkin

ISBN 978-0-944634-92-9

Published and printed in the United States of America

Introduction

In 1985 my brother, Larry, suggested the *Love and Logic Journal.* I was uncomfortable with writing articles for a new publication on a regular basis. I told him that I would soon run out of information and writing material.

The Journal was created over my protests and concerns. Much to my amazement the articles have continued to flow through my fingers, into the computer, and on to the pages. This has gone on for ten years now, and I am still a long way from running out of material.

Parents and teachers have continued to present new questions. Children have continued to present new challenges. Our research and creativity have continued to meet the challenge with new solutions.

Since we started producing the *Love and Logic Journal,* Foster W. Cline, M.D. and I have written over a hundred articles. We have written ten books and produced numerous audio and video cassettes in addition to two major Love and Logic training programs.

If anyone had told me ten years ago that I could have done that, I would have said, "Not me." In fact, every time I finished an article or book I told myself that it was my very last. I would think, "Now I have written all that I know. I have no more knowledge to share."

Yet our loyal followers and students always believed in me more than I believed in myself. As a result, I found a way to rise to the level of their belief in me to produce more and more.

This collection of articles is a celebration of what your support and encouragement has done for me. This book answers your requests that we provide all of the *Love and Logic Journal* articles from the last ten years under one cover.

These articles are living testimony to self-fulfilling prophecy:

> I don't become what I think I can,
> I don't become what you think I can,
> I become what I think you think I can.

Thank you and enjoy,

Jim Fay

Contents

SECTION ONE

Jim Fay

1

Volume 1

A Computer With a Lifetime Guarantee
Volume 1, no. 1

Barry Neil Kauffman, one of our leading psychologists, believes, "The way to change a person's behavior is to first change the way he sees his world." Kaufmann tells us that people generally do the very best they can, taking into consideration the way they see themselves and the way they see the world.

Other leading psychologists tell us the same thing in other ways. They say that our behavior is controlled by our self-concept. They say that to change a person's behavior, we must first change the self-concept. Self-concept, obviously, is very important. In fact, it is considered one of the great discoveries in psychology.

Dennis Waitley describes the importance of self-concept when he discusses two levels of the mind, the conscious and the subconscious. The conscious level functions much like a judge, collecting and evaluating information. The subconscious level functions much like a computer, storing information and making it available at a later date. The subconscious never attempts to sort out fact from fiction or truth from misperception. When information flows from the subconscious, it comes forth as fact. Therefore, all our misperceptions eventually become truth and are treated as fact by our conscious level of thinking.

Children spend monumental effort trying to understand their parents as well as their environment. They are great observers, but horrible interpreters. This is understandable, considering they have immature brains and limited experience.

But it's sad that when we become adults, all our perceptions, both accurate and inaccurate, become our reality. A child who misperceives that his parents prefer his brother does not grow up to say to his parents, "When I was young I thought you loved my brother more than me." He grows up to say, "You always liked my brother better than me." What was once his mistaken idea has now become his truth.

This says that a child is constantly observing, interpreting, and storing information in the subconscious. These billions of thoughts and experiences later become the truth that runs and directs his or her life. It is a challenge to help children interpret what they see and hear in ways that will later affirm that they are capable, lovable, and responsible.

I often wonder what misperceptions are stored in the subconscious minds of youngsters who constantly make poor decisions, involve themselves in self-destructive behavior, and who are turned off to learning. It makes me wonder how many of them misinterpreted their parents' love in the following ways:

> Some parents show their love by hovering over their child and rescuing him or her from the harsh world. The child often interprets this as, "My parents know I could never handle the world without help. I am incapable!"

> Some parents show their love through control. They constantly tell their children how to lead their lives. This is often interpreted by the child as, "My parents know that I am not capable of thinking for myself or being responsible."

I know some parents who show their love by always being available with advice. They allow their children to make many of their own decisions. This is often interpreted as, "My parents know that I can think for myself!" These children grow up to believe that somewhere within themselves is a computer with a lifetime guarantee.

In the next article, Jim shows why less control is often more.

Gain Control by Giving Some Up
Volume 1, no. 2

Many adults spend considerable energy trying to control their children. This is only natural. When we see our children out of control, it makes us feel like bad parents.

If fact, there are few things more pathetic than a child out of control. This scares parents and children alike. A child who knows that he is out of control feels insecure. He puts on a tough exterior. But his actions are easy to misread because they appear to say that he cannot and will not be controlled. He needs limits, but, at the same time, fights them.

In these situations, parents can gain control by giving away some control. A small miracle takes place when children are given alternatives rather than orders.

This technique reduces stress in families while preparing children to make decisions that affect their lives. It provides them with wonderful preparation for the adult world in which they will have to live.

Consider the following example of a parent, who, in giving some control to his child, gains more control for himself:

A youngster is making too much noise in the family room. A typical parental response might be, "Quit making so much noise! You're making me mad!" This response is usually not effective since it gives the child the wrong kind of control. He feels that he now has the power to make his parent mad.

This parent, however, gives the child some positive control over his life by offering him alternatives: "You can either stay here with us and be quiet, or go somewhere else and make noise." A determined youngster may fight this by saying, "I'm staying here! I have just as many rights as the rest of the family!" The parent's calm reply is simply, "That's not one of the options. But feel welcome to come back when you stop making noise."

Providing alternatives is based on the concept that people cannot make decisions about themselves and fight with others at the same time. Parents can easily set the limits children need by taking good care of themselves at the same time they offer alternatives.

For example, notice that the parent in this example sets limits on the child's behavior without putting him down. The youngster's dignity was maintained as he was left with a decision to make about his behavior. The parent's dignity was maintained because he handled the situation in a calm, controlled manner.

Dealing with alternatives and being held accountable for decisions is wonderful practice for youngsters. It prepares them for the lifetime of decision-making that is required of all responsible people.

Effective parents offer alternatives only if they are willing to make sure the child lives with his decisions. These parents know that children who make mistakes learn and grow. Mistakes are often better teachers than complaining parents.

*From the moment they are born, children interpret messages
that influence their self-concept. The next article presents what
parents can do to ensure their child develops a positive self-concept.*

A Tale of Two Children
Volume 1, no. 3

Once upon a time, two babies were born on the same day in the same hospital. Moments later they both went to work in an attempt to satisfy one of their life-long needs: feeling accepted and being noticed in a positive way.

Neither of these babies could understand the words their parents spoke. Each had yet to translate the language used by their loved ones. But both used a far more powerful tool. They watched their parents closely and learned to read nonverbal language. Soon they were able to notice even the most minute changes in facial expression, body tone, and tone of voice.

Over the next five years, one of these children, Sam, picked up all kinds of messages that said he was capable, lovable, and valuable. The signals from his parents said, "We love you the way you are, because you are you."

Sam was also given many opportunities to make decisions about his own life. His parents often asked him questions such as, "Do you want to wear your coat today or carry it?" They did this because they loved him and wanted the best for him.

The other child, George, picked up many signals that told him that he did not measure up to his parents' expectations. His parents' messages said, "We could give you a lot more love if you would just do better." His parents also often ordered him around: "You get that coat on. You're not going out without it!" They did this because they loved him and wanted the best for him.

The big day in these two children's lives finally arrived — the first day of school. Each had different thoughts. Sam had few doubts about his ability while George had many questions in his mind about how well he would do.

We now add a third character to our story. Miss Hush is a loving, caring and dedicated teacher. Like all of us, Miss Hush grew up with the same need to be recognized and accepted. She also spent her early years learning to read the nonverbal messages of those around her. She is an expert, but like Sam and George, she gives little conscious thought to these nonverbal messages.

Miss Hush now prepares an assignment for the class. It is passed out and all students are told what to do. Sam, who believes in himself, is quick to start the assignment and give it his best shot. George, not too sure of himself, is more tentative. He holds back. He stalls. He needs encouragement. A little voice in his head says, "You may not do as well as others. Watch out! You are going to be hurt."

The difference in performance between these two boys does not go unnoticed by Miss Hush. On the conscious level of thinking, she notices that one of them is not as capable as the other. However, she also picks up another message on the unconscious level: "Sam is going to help satisfy my need to feel like a good teacher. George is not."

Research shows that the behavior of teachers is influenced by messages at an unconscious level. Sam is going to receive more winks, nods, smiles, eye contact, touches, questions and nonverbal encouragement. If Sam ever has trouble answering a question, Miss Hush will probably think she did not ask a good question and then restate it. In her mind, she believes that Sam knows the answer. Sam will also receive more time and patience because of this.

At the same time, George receives just the opposite treatment. He receives fewer nods, smiles, touches, and less eye contact. When he falters in answering questions, Miss Hush "backs off," giving him less time to answer. She will probably not restate the question. She does not want to embarrass him.

Does Miss Hush's behavior go unnoticed by George? Absolutely not. He is busy reading nonverbal language in his constant attempts to "check out" his level of acceptance by others. He soon picks up on the message, "I'm not a student. Sam is the student. I'm not accepted by the teacher. Sam is."

George is now hurting. His self-concept is beginning to slip at a faster rate. He has to face his reality for 180 school days this year. He begins to find ways to avoid the pain by refusing to do his assignments. This gets him into trouble, so he learns many avoidance techniques.

Several years go by. George has perfected his avoidance skills. He finds other ways to be noticed. He is now labeled a behavior problem. He is considered a child who is unmotivated.

George's sixth grade teacher complains to the principal, "Why do I have to have kids like this in my class? He doesn't care about anything. He makes my life miserable and keeps me from teaching the curriculum. Why can't I have more kids like Sam? He's always a good student."

What has happened? The dreams of one of our characters have been shattered. George's self-concept has gradually slipped. He has been reinforced on a daily basis that he is not as good as the others. His teachers have constantly picked up messages from him that say, "I'm not the one to help you feel like a good teacher." At the same time, Sam, who already believes in himself, has gone through school constantly receiving cues that bolster his self-concept.

The research of Purkey, Combs, the Pennsylvania Department of Education, and many others supports the premise that many children experience a dramatic decline in enthusiasm for school between kindergarten and sixth grade. The problem is directly related to an erosion of self-concept.

It is critical to note that the underlying problem with these children is not one of motivation. Purkey has proven that almost all people are motivated in some area. Motivation is a problem only to a small percentage of students. In the majority of cases, the problem is one of a negative self-concept.

George's self-concept is like a dictator who lives in his subconscious mind. It is the ultimate authority in this life. It is constantly talking to him with words such as, "Who do you think you are? You don't do things like that. The other kids do things like that. You'll look bad and feel bad. Try to avoid it if you can."

In contrast, Sam's self-concept is always saying, "Sure, you can do it. Go for it. You'll feel great when it's over."

In some cases, there is a happier ending to our story. In each one of our schools, there is a teacher who has a special treat waiting for George. She is the teacher who believes that her job is to discover in George something that he did not know was there. She makes sure that he gets the same number of winks, nods, smiles, etc., that Sam does. She also places high expectations on him.

This teacher spends much more time noticing what George does right than what he does wrong. She will probably say, "I notice you're not doing your math, and I hope you'll get with it. But I noticed what beautiful pictures you draw. Will you draw one especially for me that I can keep at home? I always want to remember you."

George will fall in love with his teacher. He will try just a little harder to do as she asks, and he will be a little more careful about the way he behaves in her class. He will probably draw more than one picture for her as he places a new value on his drawing and looks at himself in a little more positive way.

His problems won't be solved, but he is beginning to discover a new George. He will never forget this teacher. She has done for him what no one else was willing or able to do.

The End . . . or is it?

If you're tired of getting the brush-off from your kids about school,
read the next article!

↵⌐

Teaching Kids to Withhold Information About School
Volume 1, no. 4

You're on your way home from work. You're anxious for a little encouragement, some relaxation, and maybe something cool to drink. It's been a hard day. You need all the support you can get to recharge your batteries and feel strong enough to face tomorrow.

You are greeted with, "Hi, honey. How was it today? Where are your papers? I want to see how you did today."

"It was OK. I really don't want to talk about it. Is there anything cool to drink? I'm really beat."

"Well, no wonder you don't want to talk about it. Look at these papers. You can do a lot better than this. Where was your mind today? You sit down right now and we'll go over these proposals you wrote and get the spelling straightened out. Look at these paragraphs! You'll never get promoted at this rate. I don't understand this. You have so much more potential than this!"

How long would it be before you found a more comfortable place to go after work? "Who needs this?" you'll say. "I'll find someone who can show me a little more appreciation for my hard work!"

Many school age children face this same type of situation daily. After school, they are greeted with, "What did you learn today?" and "Where is your homework? You get on it right now!"

Children are also requested to bring home their papers so that their mistakes can be corrected. This is done in the name of love and caring by parents who believe they should show an interest in their child's progress.

But children can't choose to go somewhere else after school. They can't avoid facing a replay of their daily failures at work. They must return home and listen to whatever their parents have to say.

It is very difficult for a child to say, "Mother! Do you realize you are training me to keep my school progress a secret from you?" Adults, on the other hand, spend little time with people who remind them of their failures or weaknesses.

Many parents "train" their children to avoid talking about school through the following tried-and-true method. First, the kids quit bringing home their school papers. They make excuses and blame it on their teachers. "She never gives me my papers to bring home."

Next, the parent goes to school demanding that the teacher develop some sort of foolproof reporting method, such as daily or weekly reports. This never provides a long-term solution because it addresses the wrong problem. It also robs teachers of valuable teaching and preparation time.

The real problem is that the child does not feel safe discussing school with the parent. Instead of a reporting plan, it is much wiser for parents and children to learn how to talk to each other in safe and supportive ways. This solution works and it lasts for a lifetime.

You can teach your child to want to discuss school with you. At the same time, you can lay the foundation for helping your youngster become a true winner. This technique is based on extensive research on winners and losers. Winners always think about how they are going to succeed, while losers always think about their possible failures.

Here are four steps to follow that will teach your child to discuss school with you:

Step One

Sit down with your child two to three times per week. Have him point out the best things he did on his papers.

Step Two

Make sure your child describes the reasons for her success. As she puts these into words, they become imprinted on her brain, never to be erased. She will start to believe that she is in control of her own success or failure.

Step Three

Work with your child on mistakes only when you're asked to help. Let the school work on the deficiencies. Unfortunately, many school personnel have more expertise in what's wrong than what's right. Your child will get enough attention about that at school.

Step Four

Be patient. This is a real change in operation. It will take the child a period of time to believe that it is not just a new phase you are going through.

Look for the results and benefits to show up in several months or maybe the next few years, depending upon the child's past history. One thing we do know for sure is how the old way works. We can always go back to fighting with our children and blaming teachers if we lose either our patience or our faith.

2

Volume 2

Reasoning with Children
Volume 2, no. 1

I don't know what's wrong with that child. He never listens to a thing I tell him. I might as well be talking to the wall for all he cares!" Does this sound familiar? How do we get our children to listen and benefit from our experience and knowledge? Maybe it's asking too much.

Or is it? As I look back on my own childhood, I realize I didn't do a very good job of listening to my parents. And very few of my friends listened to their parents as they should have.

We could blame this problem on the fact that kids are just headstrong and determined to learn the hard way. It's also possible that many parents try to reason with their kids at the wrong time. This "bad timing" greatly reduces the odds of success.

The wrong time to reason with a child

I've watched many parents, including myself, give their children a "good talking to" with little or no positive results. It was obvious that the adult not only had good intentions, but good advice as well. The only trouble was that the child was not in a receptive emotional state that would allow him/her to listen and make use of the adult's wisdom.

Use actions with only a few words

The words we use with our children when they are in an emotional state are wasted. They are either never heard, or they are turned against us. We all have difficulty listening during emotional times. It is natural to focus most of our energy and thoughts on the emotions rather than the words that are being spoken. As a result, we tend to remember the other person's anger more than what he or she said.

The following dinner table scene provides a good example: Georgie complains about his food and does not eat. He is reminded to eat his dinner several times without any results.

One parent might use anger and lecture to handle this situation. "What's wrong with you? How many times have I told you that this is not a cafeteria! I can't be fixing just what you want all the time. Why can't you be like your brother? Don't you dare come to this table with that attitude. I'm putting the food away and you won't get to eat until breakfast. Maybe next time you'll pay attention to me!"

Another parent might handle this situation by allowing the child to experience the natural consequence of his behavior. This parent replaces anger with empathy and understanding: "We'll be picking up the food and the dishes in five minutes. I hope by then you'll have eaten all you need to hold you until breakfast."

The youngster does not eat and nothing is said about it. Five minutes later, the food is removed and the child is sent on his or her way in a friendly manner.

Later, the child will probably say, "I'm hungry. What can I have to eat?"

This wise parent knows that the fewer words she uses, the more her child will learn. Her response is, "I bet you are. That's what happens to me when I miss my dinner. I bet you'll be anxious for breakfast. Don't worry, we'll cook a big one."

Lectures with anger cause children to think about our anger. On the other hand, consequences with empathy cause children to think about their lives and their decisions. The youngster in the second situation will probably think long and hard about the consequence. The child in the first situation will probably think more about how angry he is with his parent.

Use words when the child is in the thinking state

The best time to reason with a child is when both the child and parent are happy. A good time might be in the car when all is going well. As I look back upon my life, most of the wisdom I gained from my Dad came from what he shared with me during our happy times.

*The next article explores how to help our children
think for themselves by giving them the right kind of power.*

↩

Pulling the Tooth of Wisdom
Volume 2, no. 2

Many youngsters lose much of their personal power during the first few years of life. This is sad, because what they lose has considerable impact on their productivity as well as the quality of their life in later years. I am referring to their creative abilities and their ability to feel in control of their destiny.

Many loving parents, in their zeal to raise good children, start this "extraction process" by placing their demands in the wrong place. While we have the right to demand responsible behavior from our children, often this demand is for blind obedience. There is a critical difference between the two.

Parents demand responsible behavior by providing their children with advice and a range of choices that carry consequences. This forces their children to think for themselves. It sends the message that whoever owns the problem can solve it, and places a high value on creative thought.

Other parents use threats, intimidation, and commands to coerce their children into doing as they are told. They indicate that their way is the only acceptable way. This type of parenting conditions children to believe that others have the answers to their problems. Children in these situations are actually penalized when they think for themselves. They soon learn that thinking does not pay. What happens when children are the subject of parental threats and demands?

One
Children in these situations focus on the wrong kind of power. As they grow up, they soon try to obtain power the same way as their parents.

Two
Before long, children copy they ways their parents get power — mainly through threats, intimidation, or force. But this just makes their parents angry. It is very hard on us as adults when someone mirrors our behavior, especially that behavior we dislike about ourselves!

Three
Control is too valuable a commodity for children to give up without a fight. Unfortunately, the fight for control is not about the ability to think for oneself, but about children stubbornly trying to get their own way.

Four
Children learn through their parents' actions that they are not capable of thinking for themselves. This concept is often reinforced after they make a mistake: "See! You should have listened to me," the parent says.

What is worse, children are being trained to listen to their peers when they reach adolescence. This training takes place during a child's first eleven years when, he is in the concrete thinking stage.

By the time children learn to think abstractly, they have already been conditioned to listen to a strong voice outside their head that tells them what to do. When they reach adolescence, they no longer want to listen to this voice. A teen might say, "I can think for myself!"

That would indeed be nice. But eleven years of conditioning only leaves the child in a position to listen to another voice from the outside—that of his peers.

My job as a parent
I believe my assignment as a parent is to take a totally dependent little baby and gradually help him develop into a totally independent adult. I am usually given eighteen years to get this job done. I know of no better way to do this than to make my home as much like the real world as possible.

The real world is a place where people are constantly faced with decisions. A child preparing to live in this world needs lots of practice making these decisions and then living with the consequences. It's way too late to wait until a youngster is eighteen!

Wise parents start this process early by giving their children choices that have fairly simple consequences. They gradually move on to more complex decisions and consequences. These parents teach their children that they have the power to make their lives pleasant or not. This is known as the development of judgment and wisdom.

This approach also builds strength in children by allowing them to struggle. Recent studies indicate that children who have been denied the right to struggle in their early years are at a high risk for suicide and other self-destructive behavior. Children who are given the opportunity to struggle and overcome adversity learn that they are in control of the quality of their lives and destiny.

Parents who practice giving choices and consequences receive a pleasant surprise: they discover that they actually have more control over their children than those parents who boss their kids around. Children who are constantly trying to make decisions, especially ones that carry consequences, are often too busy thinking to fight with their parents. They also know that their parents are not trying to "extract the tooth of wisdom."

In the next article, you'll learn some easier ways to set limits for your child.

مہ

Love Me Enough to Set Limits
Volume 2, no. 3

"My kids are always trying me out. I wish for once that they would just mind without all these hassles."

"Sometimes I think she does bad things just to get me to punish her."

"I want my kids to love me. If I don't give them what they want, I worry that they'll rebel against me."

These kinds of statements are usually related to problems about reasonable and firm limits for children.

I recently watched two youngsters and their mother in a grocery store. The children were busy driving their mother to distraction while she responded with one threat after another. Each threat was more severe than the last, but still had no effect. They ranged from, "I'll slap your hands!" to "You'll never go shopping with me again!" This poor mother finally bought the children off with candy to get some peace of mind.

Children do need firm limits. Limits, in fact, are the foundation of security. Children who have limits placed on them in loving ways are fortunate. They are then secure enough to learn how to deal effectively with others as well as with their own emotions. They are easier to teach, spend less time acting out, and usually have a high degree of self-confidence.

Many children misbehave in a desperate attempt to get their parents to set limits. It's almost as if they were saying, "Don't you love me? How bad do I have to act before you will set some limits for me?"

As an explanation, I like to think of myself as sitting in a totally dark room where I can't see my hand in front of my face. My only security is my chair. I eventually muster up enough nerve to feel around in the room and move away from the chair. I will feel some degree of security if I am lucky enough to find four solid walls.

Once I test these walls and find they are strong, I will at least feel safe enough to begin exploring the rest of the room. But what if I test the walls and they crumble or fall? I will run back to my chair for security. I will no longer feel safe enough to explore very far.

Children find themselves in a similar situation as they begin learning and exploring. The world is like the dark room and the chair represents the mother figure.

Have you ever noticed that when children are afraid, they always run back to their mothers for an injection of confidence? Have you ever noticed that some parents provide walls in the form of firm limits? And, have you ever noticed that other parents leave their children feeling insecure and afraid by providing fewer limits or ones that crumble easily?

Setting firm limits is a gift of love. The problem is that we often find it difficult to set limits. Our children fight limits to see if they are firm enough to provide security. This is often misinterpreted by adults to mean we are doing the wrong thing. Kids may test us by telling us that we are mean, unreasonable, or don't love them. At this point, many parents become afraid and change the limits.

Setting limits shouldn't be confused with telling a child what to do. Orders do not set limits. They only encourage battles. Consider the following order, which encourages a child to be late just to test the limits: "You be home at 6:00 P.M. or you won't get any dinner!"

Instead, try, "I'll be serving dinner tonight at 6:00. But don't worry. I'll also be serving breakfast at the regular time if things don't work out for you." This leaves the youngster with much more to think about: "It doesn't sound as if Mom is going to serve a special meal for me if I'm late."

Most parents are pleasantly surprised at the results when they describe what they plan to do instead of telling their child what to do.

Avoid telling the child what to do:

"You're not going to talk to me like that in my own house!"
(fighting words)

Try stating what you are willing to do:

"I'll be willing to listen to you when your voice is as soft as mine." Or,
"I'll be willing to discuss that when no name calling is taking place."
(thinking words)

~

Avoid telling a child what he or she can't do:

"You can't drive the family car until you pay the insurance!" (fighting words)

Try stating what is allowed:

"Feel free to start driving as soon as you have the insurance paid."
(thinking words)

Avoid telling what you won't do:
"I'm not giving you any more allowance just because you wasted yours already!" (fighting words)

Try stating what you will do:
"Don't worry, Sweetie. You'll have some money when your allowance comes on Saturday." (thinking words)

৴৹

Limits are often set by offering choices. Think about the mother in the grocery store. She would gain more control next time by asking her children, "Would you guys rather go shopping with me and keep your hands to yourself today, or you would rather use some of your allowance to hire a babysitter to stay with you at home?"

She could give this a try. If it doesn't work, at least she will know what the children want to do next time there is a shopping trip. I bet she will take good care of herself by having the children hire their own sitter. They will know that she has established some limits, and she will probably enjoy herself for a change.

Yes, teenagers can be a joy to have around!
If you don't believe it, read the next article.

৴৹

Teenagers Are Not for Fighting
Volume 2, no. 4

"Those kids will be the death of me. How will they ever be able to live on their own? They'd lose their heads if they weren't attached at the shoulder! I'm scared to death every time they leave the house. And I spend so much time worrying that they won't come home at a decent hour. Whatever happened to the nice little kids who used to confide in me and were so much fun to have around? If I'd known it was going to be this hard, I wouldn't have had any kids!"

It's not uncommon to hear parents of teenagers talking this way. Given the pressures, temptations, and opportunities available to young people in today's world, raising a teenager is no easy task. Yet certain styles of parenting can make our job much easier and even fun.

The parent's real job
As I stated earlier, I believe my job as a parent is to help a totally dependent little baby gradually develop into a totally independent adult. I am usually given 18 years to get that job done. I am on target if I allow more and more independence so that the child makes most of his or her own decisions during the last three years in the home.

The best way to do this is by running your home like the real world. You provide your child with opportunities to practice decision-making and then live with the consequences of those decisions — both good and bad. Wise parents start this process early by giving choices that have fairly minor consequences. They gradually move on to choices with more severe or complex consequences. These parents teach their children that they have personal power over their destiny.

This approach also builds strength by allowing the child to struggle. Research shows that children who are denied the right to struggle in their early years are at a high risk for suicide and other self-destructive behaviors. Children who are allowed to struggle and overcome adversity learn that they are much more in control of the quality of their lives.

Demand responsible behavior, not blind obedience

It is our responsibility to expect and demand responsible behavior. But some parents confuse this with demanding that their child do exactly as told. This "hooks" the youngster's natural desire to have control and usually results in a battle. Sad but true, this battle is always fought over who will win control rather than the issue of responsible behavior.

Parents engaged in this kind of battle indicate that their way is the only way. They are teaching their children the same thing. Before long, the youngster has learned to act just like the adult. They say, "There is only one way and it's my way!" The parents then become afraid of losing control, and the child learns the hard way that the biggest and oldest always hold the power.

Control is too valuable a commodity for children to give up easily. They become very determined and the fight rages on. The fight is no longer about being able to think, but about how to get their own way. Unfortunately, this requires stubborn behavior rather than creative thinking.

Our job is not to demand blind obedience, but to demand careful thought, problem-solving and responsible behavior. This is more often achieved by either offering the youngster a number of choices or asking questions about what he or she thinks will be best. The following dialog is an example.

The "you be home on time!" battle

The following approach, which involves questions, answers and possible consequences, has been found to be much more effective than the "you be home on time!" battle. Be sure to provide a consequence if your teen does not show responsible behavior.

Mom: "Where are you going tonight?"

Janice: "Oh, just out."

Mom: "That's great, as long as you remember our agreement that you get to choose where you're going as long as I know where I can find you in an emergency. I'll always do the same for you. What time should I start worrying if you don't return?"

Janice: "Yeah, Mom. I'll be at the skating rink."

Mom: "Great! Be sure to give me a call if you change your plans. What time did you say you'd be in?"

Janice: "I don't know. Maybe 12:00."

Mom: "Will that give you enough time? If so, please set my alarm clock for 12:00. Your job will be to sneak in and turn it off before then so it doesn't ruin my sleep for the evening. If it does go off and you haven't called to let me know that you've changed plans, I'll know to start worrying or call for some help for you."

Teens who are given a degree of control in this manner are much less apt to demand total control by coming in later than they agreed to.

On the other hand, demanding that a teen be in at a certain time only sets up a control battle. The only way the teenager can feel independent is by being late. The adult always loses!

In the event your youngster sets a time to be home, but later calls to say, "Don't worry about me. I'll be home at 1:00 instead of 12:00," be sure to say, "Thank you!"

My dad trained me not to call home. The first time I thought I was going to be late, I called home and he jumped down my throat: "You get home this minute or there's going to be more trouble than you can take!" He also lectured me when I got home.

It didn't take me long to figure out that I got two scoldings if I called home and only one if I waited until I got home. My poor dad had to worry about me many times after this because he didn't know how to thank me for being considerate with a phone call.

Be sure to have a consequence ready if your youngster keeps you up some night by not calling if he has changed plans. The next time he says he is going out, simply say, "Oh, not tonight please. I just don't have the energy to worry about you. Feel free to go out another night when I have gotten over losing the sleep I lost last time you were out." This always works better than the reverse, which is, "You're not going out because you came home late last time."

Another consequence is also available. Remember that no teen can live in a family without help from his/her parents. My mother taught me this when I once asked her to iron my pants for a dance. Her reply was, "Ordinarily I'd be happy to. But I'm so tired from worrying about you last night and losing sleep that I'm just not up to it right now. Try me again sometime when I've had more sleep."

I tried to iron my pants, burned a hole in them, and said, "See what you made me do!" But it did me no good because she answered, "That's an interesting way to look at that. I'm sorry it worked out that way." I did a lot of thinking that evening!

Parents who allow their kids to make many decisions and who are there to provide genuine sorrow for them when the consequences are negative find that their youngsters become more independent and a joy to be around!

3

Volume 3

The Gift of Struggle
Volume 3, No. 1

Are we stealing from our children? Is it possible that we could be sabotaging our own efforts to make things better for our kids? If so, I'm sure that this arises out of our loving desire to help our children. In our attempts to be good parents, we often take away a youngster's opportunity to struggle. This leaves the child vulnerable to underachievement and at a high risk for suicide.

Schools today face an epidemic of underachievers. These are children who cannot, or will not put out the effort needed to succeed at school. These children express their reluctance to work in a variety of ways. Some say they are bored. Others say that the work is irrelevant, too difficult or too easy. They often appear confused, stressed or even incapable of doing more. Regardless of how they describe it, they are not willing to pay the price of academic success.

Many of these children find their way into special classes for the learning disabled where teachers pull their hair out trying to figure out the problem. These teachers soon discover they are not working with a learning disability, but with a self-concept problem. In others words, these children believe with all their hearts that they are incapable of doing the work being asked of them.

A child with a low self-concept is unwilling to do school work because of the possibility of failure. It is not unusual for the youngster to give the impression that the adults are applying too much pressure and need to back off.

Well-meaning teachers often suggest that the parents be more understanding, supportive and helpful with homework. Sometimes this helps. But more often it is the worst possible suggestion.

It is not uncommon to find that the same child has similar problems at home. The youngster has learned at an early age that the adults will rescue him when the going gets tough. This often happens when loving parents are too quick to help with homework or to solve their child's problems. Children quickly become addicted to their parent's attention and help and actually begin believing the unstated message that they cannot succeed on their own.

This problem was not as severe years ago. Parents were preoccupied with the depression, World War II, scratching out a living, and were in need of help from their children. Youngsters had more responsibilities because they were forced to contribute to the family's survival. Because they had to struggle to get the job done at home, they were prepared to struggle at school.

Today's underachievers often have parents who had to struggle when they were children. "I don't want my kids to struggle like I did. I want a better life for them," they say. They often move to the extreme in their attempts to make things better for their children.

How sad this is. Children who did not learn how to struggle are not able to make the effort necessary to succeed at school. Even sadder are recent studies that show that children denied the opportunity to struggle during their early years are at a high risk for suicide. They simply are not able to see themselves solving problems when the need arises. They are only able to see one way out.

Solutions

The primary solution to this problem is to give children more responsibility. This can be done by making chores a top priority for our children.

We prepare our children for the real world be being consistent in our expectations about chores. The most effective way to do this is by saying, "There's no hurry on the chores. I just want them completed before your next meal."

It is far less damaging to a child to go without a meal than to avoid the struggle of finishing the chore. A missed meal has short-term implications, while avoiding struggle has serious long-term effects that reduce self-concept.

I was recently asked if this should also apply to a teenager who has a lot of homework, school activities, and a part-time job. Teenagers are experts in believing they have more important things to do than mundane chores. They even decide that studying is more important.

My answer was, "Absolutely! The chores come first!" Say to your youngster, "I hope you learn to do your chores fast enough so that the rest of your activities don't have to suffer."

Sylvia B. Rimm, Ph.D., author of *Underachievement Syndrome,* tells us that many children's learning problems at school are solved when parents increase their expectations for the completion of tasks at home. She also tells us that children develop self-confidence through struggle. One of her 12 rules for helping underachievers is: "Children feel more tension when they are worrying about their work than when they are doing their work."

In the next article, Jim explains
why underachievement problems need to be solved on the home front.

Don't Shoot the Teacher!
Volume 3, no. 2

Some children are conditioned to underachieve before they even enter school. Their teachers and parents often spend years of frustration trying to get them to reach their potential. They are often disappointed by these bright children who seem to want to achieve, but just can't seem to put out the effort necessary to succeed. It almost appears as if they have learned to avoid the very thing they need to do to be successful learners.

It is so easy to blame the school. These statements from frustrated parents are not uncommon:

"If only the teacher could be more understanding."
"The school just doesn't have the necessary discipline."
"If the school would just go back to the basics . . . "

In reality, many learning-related problems do not start in school and cannot be cured with more discipline, more understanding on the part of teachers, or more time spent on the basics. School improvement efforts should be directed toward the achievement problems that are created by the school. However, no amount of change in the school system will solve the underachievement problems that start in the home.

There are a number of family patterns that condition children to become underachievers. Sylvia B. Rimm, Ph.D., author of *Underachievement Syndrome*, lists 15 different achievement problems that can be traced directly to attitudes and beliefs that children develop before they ever meet their first teacher. These attitudes and beliefs are the products of relationships the children have had with their parents.

Let's look at one of these situations. But first, we must recognize that the problems we create for our children are usually born out of our love for them, and the fact the none of them ever arrive at our doorstep with an instruction manual!

We therefore tend to look back on how we were raised, saying to ourselves, "I hope to continue what was good about the way I was raised and correct what was bad." But we usually overcompensate and change what was not good into something opposite — but still not so good.

Many people who experienced a lot of pain as a child devote their adult lives to insulating their own children from pain. They later learned that this just caused different kinds of problems for their children. In other words, they traded bad for bad.

Consider the following situation in which one parent had to struggle for what she got as a youngster. As an adult, she is dedicated to making sure her child does not experience the same pain. Her husband believes it is best for children to earn what they get. These differing opinions provide the potential for a family pattern that could lead their child to become an underachiever.

In this type of family, the child usually figures out how to get what he or she wants. This first requires a visit with Dad. "Daddy, I need some more money because my allowance ran out," pleads Rachel. You can guess what this type of father answers: "That's sad. You'll have to wait until Saturday for your regular allowance or find a way to earn some money."

Next, Rachel goes to mother: "Mom, look how mean Daddy is! He won't help me!" Mother, who is dedicated to making sure Rachel experiences no pain, finds herself saying, "Now, now. Don't worry. Daddy's just tired and doesn't understand. I'll get you some money, but be sure not to tell him."

I am sure this mother is hoping to show that she is loving, concerned, and a good friend. The sad truth is that the foundation for underachievement has just been laid. Yes, the child may see mother as loving, but a devastating lesson has also been taught: you don't get want what you want through effort. You get what you want through manipulation.

You can be sure this attitude will be firmly set by the time the Rachel goes to school. You can guess what the youngster will think when the teacher says, "Here's some school work. It will take some effort on your part to learn it." This poor child will think, "No way! Effort is not the way you get what you want. There is always an easier way."

It won't be long before Rachel explains her poor grades to her parents by saying, "Look how mean the teacher is. She just doesn't understand!" This may seem so sincere that we soon find she has manipulated both parents into joining her against the school and teacher. The child now has more power than either the parent or the teacher.

The parents are often confused—first blaming the school, then blaming the child, then blaming the school, all with no success in getting the child to live up to her promise.

All kinds of ideas are used to get the child to put out some effort. They include daily reports from the school, more homework, rewards, punishments, school conferences, labels such as "learning disabled," and even special education classes as a way of explaining the problem.

None of these work because they are not the reasons behind the child's lack of effort and achievement. The problem is solved when both parents understand the need for a consistent set of expectations for their child. "We both want the best for you and know this will come from effort, not from manipulating one of us against the other."

These parents need to get into the habit of sticking together and supporting each other when confronted with, "Look how mean your spouse is!" They might try saying, "I can see how it looks that way to you. I do hope you get it worked out."

Do you feel guilty when you say "no" to your children?
In the next article, find out why "no" doesn't have to be a four-letter word.

"No" Is Not a Four-letter Word
Volume 3, no. 3

Children need to know that their parents are able to say "no" and mean it. However, it is unusual for them to thank us for having the strength to set limits for them. Instead, they usually do all they can to test those limits.

This can be confusing. Why are our children so testy when we are doing what is best for them? Limits provide the security they need to develop self-confidence.

Those children who lack external controls often misbehave in various ways. It is their attempt to force us to provide the limits that will allow them to feel confident about their place in the world. Children with little or no external controls also often suffer from low self-esteem.

It appears that children test us to make sure that the limits are firm enough to provide the security they need. Each youngster seems to have his or her own special testing routine. Some kids use anger, some use guilt, and some are sneaky. Others prefer to forget things as a way of testing our resolve when we say "no."

I wish I could say that children will give us a vote of confidence after they have tested our limits and found them to be strong. But they never say, "Thanks, Dad. I feel a lot more secure now that I know you mean what you say. I appreciate you loving me enough to set limits."

Instead, they may pout, complain, stomp around, run to their rooms, whine, or talk back. This often leaves parents angry and confused.

It helps to remember that children hear the word "no" far too often. In fact, it has been shown that parents of two-year-olds typically say "no," in some form, about 77% of the time. No wonder our children get sick of hearing it. The word "no" just seems to be a "call to arms." In other words, "no" is a fighting word.

Youngsters often wage war against "no" in a very subtle way. They try to get the parent to do all the thinking while they stand back and judge the quality of the work. The know that parents who are busy reasoning with them have neither the time or energy to win the battles.

Caring parents feel guilty about saying "no" and are soon hooked into lots of thinking and explaining. All the youngster has to do is interrupt from time to time with, "But Dad, it's just not fair! You just don't understand." In no time, the parent, who is doing all the work, is worn down to the point of giving in: "Oh, all right. Take it! But this is the last time. Don't ask me again."

You can turn the tables on children, forcing them to do most of the thinking. This happens when you replace "no" to one thing by saying "yes" to something else. This is called using "thinking words" instead of "fighting words." Compare the two approaches in the following examples:

Fighting words: "You can't go out to play until you practice your lessons."

Thinking words: "Yes, you may go out to play as soon as you practice your lessons."

Fighting words: "You can't watch television until your chores are done."

Thinking words: "You may watch television as soon as your chores are done."

Most youngsters try to argue when confronted with "thinking words." However, you now have the ammunition to win since you started the conversation with "yes" instead of "no." You no longer need to feel guilty. And, you no longer need to justify or explain your position.

You now hold the "state-of-the-art" in arguing in your hands. No matter what your youngster says, simply agree that it is probably true. Then add the word "and" followed by your first sentence. Note the difference in the following two conversations:

Teen: "I need the car to go skiing."

Dad: "You can't use the car until you pay your gas bill."

Teen: "But Dad, I promised my friends."

Dad: "Why don't you make them drive once in a while?"

Teen: "But Dad. You don't like the way they drive. You don't want to have to worry about me, do you?"

Here, Dad is quickly losing control of the conversation. He would be more successful if he could force the teen to do all the thinking. Here's how it's done:

Teen: "I need the car to go skiing."

Dad: "Feel free to use it as soon as your gas bill is paid up."

Teen: "But Dad. I promised my friends."

Dad: "I'm sure that's true . . . and feel free to use it as soon as you get it paid."

Teen: "Yea, but then I won't have money for the lift ticket."

Dad: "I bet that's true, too . . . and feel free to use it as soon as you get it paid."

Teen: "Gee! All you can think about is money!"

Dad: "That could be true, too . . . and . . . "

Teen: "Yea, I know. Don't say it again!"

It is rewarding to discover that this technique, called negative assertion, can eliminate fights with our children. Just think how well it might work on the adults at work!

Are you often the subject of "kid attack?"
Learn the ultimate way to handle it in the next article!

The Strategic Training Session
Volume 3, no. 4

Have you ever noticed that children have an uncanny knack for knowing when their parents are vulnerable to "kid attack?" As one mother put it, "Little Susie behaves just great when we are going somewhere she wants to go. But just let it be a shopping trip for me and she goes wild! It always happens in a public place where I just can't seem to get control. Everyone stares at us and I'm always so embarrassed I could just die!"

The bad news is that this seems to happen to all of us. Children turn on their little radar sets and find ways to get the upper hand when we have the least amount of tactical support. They usually sense that we are busy and want to avoid embarrassment in public. Because of this, they often repeat the same misbehavior over and over again.

The good news is that once they have played their hand a few times, waging war in public, we can counter with our own war game. It's called the Strategic Training Session. This maneuver has brought warmth to the hearts of many a parent while helping develop happier, more responsible kids.

Our friend who told us about little Susie recently employed the Strategic Training Session with outstanding results. The first step was to call her best friend: "I've been having trouble with Susie at the store and I need your help. Would you station yourself at the pay phone outside the store tomorrow at 10:30? I have a feeling you are going to get a call." They visited on the phone and set up the Strategic Training Session.

Mother and Susie went shopping the next day. Sure enough, Susie was her usual obnoxious self. Using a quiet voice,  Mom asked, "Would you rather behave or go sit in your room?" Susie called Mom's bluff and continued to act up.

Susie then found herself being escorted to a phone where Mom was dialing and saying, "Shopping is not fun today. Please come!"

Figuring this to be a ploy, Susie continued her whining and begging. Thirty seconds later, her eyes grew very large as she saw Mom's best friend come up to her and say, "Let's go to your room. You can wait for your mother there."

Susie was taken home and sent to her room; Mother enjoyed a quiet shopping experience; and Mother's best friend watched television. Susie was allowed to come out of her room as soon as Mom came home. She appeared most happy to see her mother again. Mother was pleasant and friendly because she had enjoyed shopping alone.

Our victorious mother reports that she and her friend set up another Strategic Training Session the next day. Susie started her usual store behavior with squinty eyes and whining mouth. However, when asked about whether she would rather shape up or go to her room, her eyes suddenly became very large and her mouth became very shut.

4

Volume 4

Sassing
Volume 4, no. 1

W hat's wrong with that kid? No respect! Every time I turn around she's talking back. It seems as if she always has to have the last word. Kids today just don't respect adults like they did in my day."

This question, asked at one of my seminars, reminds me that concerns about children who "talk back" are common. Sassing is a frustrating problem to many parents.

Solving the sassing problem usually requires a behavior change in both the youngster and parent. First, I like to look at my own behavior because it is something I can control. I do this by waiting until the next time my youngster talks back. Then I ask myself, "What did I say a split second before the sassing took place?"

We often find that the child felt criticized and was reacting to this criticism. Even adults have a hard time handling criticism. In fact, criticism usually does very little good even when it is well-intended. It is difficult for me to remember a time when I reacted positively when someone said to me, "I'm only doing this for your own good."

It is a good practice to state reasonable expectations for a child. It is also a good practice to apply consequences, with empathy, when the child does not meet these expectations. Criticizing a youngster does not usually bring about any long-term behavior change. Instead, it breeds resentment and erodes self-confidence.

Explore the child's real feelings

Now that I have a handle on my own behavior and have eliminated criticism, it's time to work with the youngster. I'd like to have a little discussion, but I must remember that this is only effective when the child is happy. It does not pay to discuss problems with children when they are upset. The purpose of this talk is to encourage the child to think about his or her actions and learn new ways of talking so there is better understanding.

"Sandy, I've noticed that you often have words for me when I ask you to do things. I wonder if I'm hearing it in the same way you really mean it. I guess I'm pretty confused about what you're trying to tell me. Are you trying to say that:

> you're embarrassed,
> or that you feel put down,
> or that you want to be the boss,
> or that you hate me,
> or that you don't know a neat way to answer . . .

Does any of this sound familiar to you?"

This usually leads to some kind of discussion. It is absolutely necessary to listen without defending or judging. The reaction that works best is to say, "Thanks for sharing."

Help with problem-solving

Most kids are willing to work with us after a discussion like this. However, they are often at a loss for better ways to answer us when they are angry or embarrassed. The following type of discussion is often helpful:

> Dad: "Sandy, if I hear you right, you really don't mean to sound the way you do. So what are your thoughts on different ways to answer?"

> Sandy: "I don't know."

> Dad: "Well, that's sad. Why don't you give it some thought and let me know if you need some suggestions. I bet that you can come up with some new ideas. If not, I can tell you some of the ways that adults handle these things. Good luck!"

While the youngster is thinking it over, try to think up some suggestions to provide if necessary.

We often make progress with sassing by eliminating criticism, helping the youngster express his or her real feelings, helping the child find new words, and then by providing practice opportunities.

In the next article, read how one parent learned
to dole out equal doses of consequences and empathy.

↙⌐

Consequences + Empathy = A Powerful Message
Volume 4, no. 2

While delivering a speech recently on parenting, I heard myself say to a woman, "Why are you attending so many of my presentations? You must know everything I'm going to say even before I say it." She frequently attended my speeches and always sat in the front row.

"Well," she said, "Research says that if you want to master something, you must hear it at least six times. And since you explained to us how to listen to the Love and Logic tapes and presentations, I have learned to listen for different things each time." (When listening to Love and Logic tapes, we suggest you concentrate on one issue at a time, listen to our treatment of that subject, practice it, and master it before going to the next issue.)

"I'm working on giving consequences with empathy," she continued. "You'll be happy to know that I'm getting pretty good at making sure my children always have the control I want them to have. I'm even getting good at making sure they do more thinking than I. But the real reason I'm back is because I'm still having trouble with the part about providing empathy with consequences." (The concept of empathy with consequences forces a child to think about his or her mistakes instead of being mad at the parent.)

Step number one

I congratulated her on taking the first step—making sure her children had the control she wanted them to have. I encouraged her to keep trying—providing empathy when you are angry and upset is not easy to do. But it works like magic when you do it right.

"I almost did it last week," she said. "I was so close. My daughter didn't study her spelling. I kept hearing your voice in my head saying, 'This could be a great opportunity. Don't blow it by reminding her.'"

"You'd be proud of me, Jim. I didn't remind her. I also heard your voice saying, 'The school will provide the consequences. Then you can balance it with an equal amount of empathy.'"

I'm so sorry

"It worked out just right. She came home with a 'D' on her test, and I did a great job of feeling sorry for her. I said, 'Wow! It must really be embarrassing to get a 'D.' I bet it's hard to face your teacher when you haven't studied. I bet you feel awful.'"

"Great!" I said, getting excited about seeing one of our Love and Logic basics work again.

"Jim, it worked just like you said it would. She got real quiet and was thinking hard about what she had done. It was wonderful! Then I heard your voice in my head again saying, 'When you run out of things to say, transfer the problem to the youngster by asking a question.'"

"I did a good job on that too, saying 'Gee, what are you going to do?' That poor child was really thrown by that! I saw her thinking so hard!"

"With the saddest little face you've ever seen, she said, 'I don't know what I'm going to do.' I had her owning her own problem and thinking harder than she had in years."

Then . . . "I Blew It."

"And then . . . I just had to do it. I blew it. I don't know why, but I just blurted out, 'And since your refuse to study, you're not going to that party on Friday!'"

"That did it! She stood straight up and started yelling, 'What do you mean I'm not going to the party! It's not my fault I got a 'D!' You should see the words that teacher gives! She never gives us any time to study and she never helps me when I raise my hand and . . . and . . . and . . . it's just not fair!'"

"Well, Jim, that's why I'm back tonight. Isn't it amazing? It took only one misstatement from me to undo all my good work and change my child from a thinker to a fighter. I changed the whole focus of her anger from herself to me in one sentence. I came back to master the art of consequencing with empathy.

"If you don't see me for a while, you'll know I've finally mastered it."

After that night, I didn't see that mother for at least five or six speeches that I gave in her area. I'm guessing she finally mastered how to give her children equal parts of consequences and empathy, and that life is smoother at her house these days.

The "V" of Love, discussed in the next article,
can help parents decide how much control to give their children.

꿈

Too Much of a Good Thing
Volume 4, no. 3

As school gets underway each fall, parents all over the country take a good look at how their children measure up in responsibility and maturity compared to the previous year. As parents, our goal is to give children a certain amount of freedom and control over their lives, so that their responsibility and maturity levels increase with each passing year. The tough part is deciding how much control and freedom to give and when to give it.

Like most good things, control and freedom can be misused. Children who are given too much control at an early age are not fun to be around. In fact, they don't even like being around themselves.

When power comes too early

Children who have more control than they can handle often act out in unbelievable ways to show that they need limits. It's almost as if they're saying, "How bad do I have to act before you control me?" However, this behavior is very confusing to both the parent and child. The child, who is now addicted to power, demands more power and at the same time asks for more parental control.

This puts the parents in a double bind. They have no choice but to clamp down on the youngster and take away some of the child's control. When this happens the child feels "unfaired upon" and the war is on.

Many people say these children appear to be angry. How right they are! Children who start out with too much power force us to increase the limitations we place on them. Who wouldn't be angry? If my control was gradually being taken away, I would feel like I was being robbed of something that is rightfully mine.

"V" of Love

Dr. Sylvia Rimm offers an explanation for this problem. She reminds us that we compare the amount of control we have in a relationship to the control we used to have, not with how much we think we should have. A child who grows up with parents who give out control in increasing amounts is usually satisfied with the amount of control. Each year the child says, "Isn't this great! I have more control than I did last year."

This is known as the "V" of Love. Loving parents use the "V" as a guideline for setting limits and allowing decision-making. The sides of the "V" stand for firm limits within which the child may make decisions and live with the consequences. The bottom point of the "V" represents birth, while the top of the "V" represents the time when youngsters leave home.

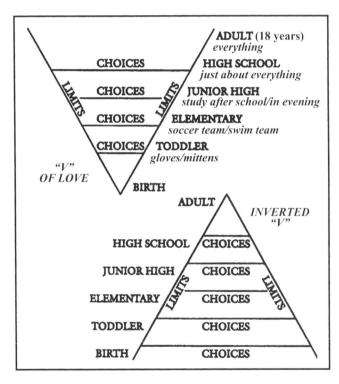

As the diagram indicates, toddlers make decisions about things such as chocolate milk or white milk. Ten-year-olds make choices about how to spend their allowance, and 17-year-olds make decisions about almost every aspect of their lives. That's the way it goes in healthy, loving families.

Upside-down "V":
Upside-down world
Unfortunately, the "V" is turned upside down in some families. In these cases, the child is treated almost like a miniature adult right from the beginning, with all the rights and privileges of adulthood.

These children soon become tyrants. We've all seen them actually controlling their parents in a variety of ways. They hold their parents hostage to temper tantrums and pouts. Our immediate thought is, "Someone needs to set limits for that kid!"

The diagram of the inverted "V" tells a sad story. It's about many unhappy children who start out with too much power. Eventually, their misbehavior forces the

"V" to be tightened. This leaves the child in a constant state of anger because of the frequent losses of privilege and control. The unhappy youngster is forever saying, "It's not fair. You're always treating me like a child."

In more severe cases, the point at the top of the "V" represents prison or a tightening of limits for the person who is addicted to power, who is angry, and who is constantly acting out. Eventually, society gives this person a fresh start at the bottom of another "V," behind bars.

At the Love and Logic Institute, we believe children should have the opportunity to make decisions. We also believe those decisions should be made within structure. In other words, adults set firm outside limits within which the child is free to make choices appropriate for his or her age.

This is easier said than done. However, it helps to keep the "V" in mind so that you always leave bigger decisions for next year, while giving the child more control this year than last.

Parents should consider talking to teachers who are often knowledgeable about age-appropriate decision-making. This can be both an interesting and rewarding discussion. Remember, too, that some of the greatest experts on parenting live in your own neighborhood. However, it's smarter to talk with parents who have well-adjusted children as opposed to those whose children are driving them crazy.

It's never too early to start offering your child choices.
Jim presents this concept in the next article.

Choices Start Early
Volume 4, no. 4

Love and Logic parents try to give their children choices instead of demands whenever possible. This way, they gain control by first giving a little control away. (The Love and Logic audio cassette, *The Science of Control*, provides the reasons behind and examples of this technique.)

"At what age can I start giving my child choices instead of orders?" is one of the most often-asked questions we receive. Foster W. Cline, M.D., co-founder of the

Love and Logic Institute, believes we should start giving them at about the same time our little ones can sit in a high chair and spit beets. Spitting food, says Dr. Cline, provides an excellent opportunity to start giving choices while setting some firm limits about dinnertime behavior.

At the Love and Logic Institute we believe that battles over food in the early years are usually fought in the subconscious mind when a person becomes an adult. Therefore, it is not wise to have a lot of rules and fights over eating. However, we do need to set some firm limits, and these must be enforced without anger and without using a lot of words.

You can effectively enforce these limits by using actions, instead of words, to offer choices to your child. As soon as your youngster spits out his or her food, the parent says, "Oh, goody, meal's over." The child is taken down from the high-chair and the food is put away. There are very few words spoken and no anger is expressed.

It only takes a few experiences like this for the average youngster to discover that there are choices to be made even when the parent doesn't explain them.

Some people disagree. "You can't reason with a child that age. Language skills are not yet developed."

What these people are really saying, says Dr. Cline, is that their children are not as smart as the family dog! He reminds us that children are smarter than dogs by the time they reach nine months old. Although a dog who has no language skills is expected to understand us without explanation, some feel a child needs to talk before he or she can comprehend our actions.

I have often seen parents and teachers try to reason with youngsters and explain what they should have learned. Have you ever seen anyone try to reason with the family German Shepherd? "Now Duke, give me some eye contact so I can tell you what you should have just learned."

It sounds ridiculous when put it into this context. In reality, we assume that the dog can learn on his own by experiencing the consequences of his behavior. However, we treat youngsters as though they are less intelligent than the dog by thinking they must be able to talk before they can learn from mistakes and consequences.

A child learns very quickly that negative behavior does not pay off. In the case of violating table rules, it only takes a few experiences for the child to learn what the choices are:

1. Eat nicely and have all you want.
2. Act out and end the meal immediately.

The child learns about choices even though the parents are not talking about them. Of course, this is only effective when the youngster does not eat until the next meal and when the parents can show sadness about the child's hunger.

Parents should not give in to their child if he or she gets hungry. The next opportunity to eat should be at the next regular meal. Parents can express their empathy by saying, "Yes, I get really hungry too if I don't eat enough when I have the chance. But don't worry, we'll be eating again soon."

5

Volume 5

The Enforcer Strikes Out
Volume 5, no. 1

How many times have you heard yourself give a hollow order you know will never be followed? Kids can't wait to hear a parental "cry in the wilderness" because they know it means you are at the end of your rope.

Each time we make a statement that cannot be enforced, we give up a little more authority. The fastest way to lose authority is to tell our child what to do and what not to do.

Compliant children often do as they are told and trick us into believing that our orders will actually work. However, resistive children quickly discover that their parents can't make them do anything, and that they win every time their parents fall into the trap of issuing orders.

Some parents avoid these problems because their word is gold. They make only those statements that can be enforced. They understand that they only have control over themselves and no one else.

The art of making enforceable statements consists of talking about ourselves and what we will allow, what we will do or what we will provide. The following examples should be helpful:

Unenforceable statement:
"Don't talk to me in that tone of voice."

Enforceable statement:
"I'll be glad to listen when your voice is as soft as mine."

Unenforceable statement:
"You get to work on your studying!"

Enforceable statement:
"Feel free to join us for some TV when you finish studying."

Unenforceable statement:
"Be nice to each other. Don't fight."

Enforceable statement:
"You're both welcome to be around me when you stop fighting."

Unenforceable statement:
"As long as you live in this house, you're not going to drink."

Enforceable statement:
"I'll be glad to let you use my car as long
as I don't have to worry about the use of alcohol."

Parents who start early making enforceable statements and then enforce them regularly raise children who believe they mean what they say. These children don't test the limits very often.

Parents who make statements that can't be enforced raise children who are constantly testing them to see if they really mean what they say.

I recently watched two different teachers handle the same problem. Each wanted the class to clean up the room before going to lunch. The first teacher said, "You are not going to lunch until this room is clean, so get to work on it right now. I mean it!"

As you can guess, only about three children started to clean. She raised her voice: "I mean everybody. Get to work!"

Nothing happened, so she said, "Look! There goes the other second-grade class. They'll be finished and out on the playground before you guys even get to lunch."

The children still didn't respond. "Oh forget it! I'll do it myself," she yelled in frustration. "I don't know what is wrong with kids today!" She lined up the class and marched them down the hall, complaining all the way to the lunchroom.

The other teacher used enforceable statements with much better results. "Hey, class," she said, "I'll be sending you to lunch as soon as the room is clean. There's no hurry."

She immediately turned her back and went to her desk where she pulled our her lunch. Then she spread her food out on the desk and began eating. As you can guess, the children were running all around the room cleaning and yelling, "Look! We're getting it. It's finished!" The teacher looked up, remarked about the wonderful job they had done and invited them to line up for lunch.

As soon as the children left, I said, "That was a masterpiece. Tell me the psychology behind why it worked."

"I'm not sure, Jim. That's just the way I've always done it," she answered.

My guess is that this teacher grew up with parents who used enforceable statements. She learned to use these kinds of statements by copying her parents' style.

Many of us weren't so lucky. We need to practice this technique often. You might say, "Hey, kids. From now on, you need to know that I will be passing out dessert to those of you who protect your teeth by brushing them." It's a lot easier to withhold treats than it is to make a youngster brush his or her teeth.

Are you a wimp?
Read how to overcome this problem beginning on the next page.

↤

Overcoming the "Wimp" Factor
Volume 5, no. 2

Will your children hate you if you insist that they act responsibly? Will they rebel if you say "no" in a firm manner? Will you damage their personalities if you say, "That's enough of that! You take that behavior off to your room! And don't come back until you can show some respect for yourself and others!"

The answer to all of these questions is absolutely not!

Is it OK for me to take a firm stand on a desired behavior? Is it OK for me to talk in a stern voice when I give choices? Is it OK for me to demand that my children pick up their things? After all, they say they live in this house, too. Is it OK for me to insist on knowing where my children are and to require them to be home at a certain time? Is it OK for me to ask my children to help with household chores—even though they're so busy?

The answer to all these questions is absolutely yes!

However, the very best answer to questions related to limits is that children feel most secure around parents who are strong. They lose respect for adults who don't set limits and make them stick. As Foster Cline says, children who act out without having to face any consequences turn into brats.

It's sad to see the number of young parents who don't take a stand with their children. They fear their children will see them as mean, unreasonable, or dictatorial. Some actually fear their children will be ruined in some way if they take a firm stand about behavior.

Our consultants all too often hear young parents describe the following dilemmas:

> "He just won't go to his room when I send him."

> "I tell her that her behavior is unacceptable, but she gets mad and throws a fit."

> "I send him to his room, but he just keeps coming out."

> "I just don't know what to say to him when he hits me and throws things at me."

It doesn't hurt a child in any way when a parent speaks in a firm voice. However, it is important to make sure your voice sounds firm, not angry. I often see parents trying to be firm, but their voices and faces display anger and rejection. The child is left confused about whether the parent is being mean or trying to be firm and just not quite pulling it off.

The only thing the child learns is that the parent feels helpless. Helpless parents in turn leave their children with a sense of unhealthy power. This is not only scary, but leads children to feelings of intense insecurity.

Insecure children act out to get their parents to set limits. It is almost as if they're saying, "How bad do I have to act to get you to set some limits for me?"

It's important to understand that the wimp factor has little to do with our words and a lot to do with our tone of voice and body language. These are both ruled by our own fears and expectations. If we're afraid our children won't behave, or that we have no right to ask them to behave, it will show in our voices and body language. The child will read the voice but not the words.

The first step in eliminating the wimp factor is to come to grips with your right as a parent to demand responsible behavior. If you have any doubts about this, refer to the first two paragraphs of this article.

The second step is to believe that you are truly capable of getting your child to respond. This usually happens when a parent discovers a new technique, such as the ones presented in the Love and Logic audio cassettes, *The Science of Control* and *Setting Limits for Kids*.

These tapes encourage parents either to provide choices with which the child must live, or that the parents use enforceable statements, such as, "I'll be glad to discuss that with you when your voice is calm."

Additional techniques can be found in two Love and Logic books, *Tickets to Success* and *Helicopters, Drill Sergeants & Consultants*.

The third way to overcome the "wimp" factor is by believing that your child wants to respond. Once more, this comes gradually as you see the child responding to your new techniques.

Our work at the Love and Logic Institute shows that, with the exception of the seriously disturbed, children do want to feel good, helpful, and cooperative. It is our negative techniques that most often bring out their resistance.

How to portray the "wimp" factor

You've seen other parents "wimp out." What do they look like? They usually lack a strong body posture, they do not look their child in the eye, and their voices often tremble or quiver.

Even if these characteristics are only slight, they are enough to tell a child, who is finely tuned to this sort of thing, that the parent doesn't mean business. They also tell the child that the parents are unsure of their demands and personal rights.

Practice the calm, firm approach

Parents are encouraged to rehearse new techniques mentally before trying them out on their children. This is especially helpful in overcoming the wimp factor.

The first time you pull off a new technique should be when you have the time, when you have the energy, when you have someone to support your actions, and when you have practiced it in your mind to the point where you can't wait for you children to give you a chance to try it out! Mentally practice the following until you feel comfortable:

Step One

Pick the situation and what you want the child to do.

Step Two

Picture yourself standing tall, looking directly into your child's eyes, and feeling you have a perfect right to expect what you are about to request. Check yourself in the mirror.

Step Three

Imagine the sound of your voice.

Step Four

Try the new technique out on a friend and get his or her opinion.

Step Five

Rehearse this until you hear yourself say, "Kid, make my day!"

Will your children get angry and try to test you when you try out new techniques? Probably. Your youngster will most likely try anything to get you back into your old behavior. It isn't unusual for children to feel frustrated, claim unfairness, or say that you don't love them.

I have known children actually to say, "What happened to the nice parent I used to have?" Once you hear this, you know you are starting to be successful. Keep up the good work!

Shopping with your children is possible. Read how in the next article.

∽

Don't Touch!

Volume 5, no. 3

I hate to go shopping. I've hated it for as long as I can remember. A number of people have tried to help me with my problem by saying, "What's the matter with you? I don't understand why you can't learn to enjoy shopping as much as I do." None of this has helped me like shopping any better.

I had a flashback the other day in a Montgomery Ward store. It gave me a chance to gain some insight into my problem. I was coping with yet an another shopping excursion by watching some parents trying to handle their children. Suddenly I heard a slap followed by the sound of a screaming parent:

"How many times have I told you not to touch? Do you want to go to the restroom for another spanking? You must have thought the last one was a picnic. Well, let me tell you that next time is not going to be fun! I'll give you a spanking you won't forget! Don't make me tell you one more time to keep your hands off things. Don't touch. I mean it!"

There was the flashback. I could see myself 50 years ago in Thrifty Drug Store in Los Angeles. I was going through the store, doing what little kids do, trying to be big by doing what big people do.

The adults touched and examined the merchandise. So I touched and examined the merchandise. Then I got yelled at and my hands were slapped. I was embarrassed in front of all the patrons of Thrifty Drug.

What a confusing situation for a child. I was acting in natural ways, learning how to be big by copying the adults. But I didn't get to feel big. What I got was punishment, embarrassment and humiliation.

Experiences like these are soon pushed deep into our subconscious because they are painful. However, they are always a part of our personal feelings and reactions.

Now when my wife, Shirley, invites me to go shopping, I don't say, "No thanks. I had a painful experience around shopping when I was a child." Instead, I just feel a low level of anxiety about shopping and try to avoid it at all costs. For some reason, it's easy to feel the anxiety and difficult to remember the painful experiences that create it.

Human beings, by nature, are "copying" animals. This means we learn best by watching others and imitating their behavior. That's one reason we have so many of the same habits, values, and mannerisms as our parents.

This imitation happens on the subconscious level. We are never actually aware of it taking place. Psychologists call it learning through modeling.

These thoughts lead me to be more and more aware of the reasons behind many shopping battles. They can often be traced back to the issue of modeling. Children are trying to be grown up, and their parents are frustrated by this.

How often have you seen a small child, in his determination to be big, refuse to hold the hand of his parent while walking? I don't even need to describe the ensuing battle. And how often have you seen a little person try to be independent by walking out in front of his parents, only to be yelled at in public?

I often wonder how much spanking and humiliation goes on across the nation each day as children examine merchandise in the stores. Yet there is a solution:

Step One

Teach the your children to act in independent yet responsible ways. For instance, many parents teach their children how to be responsible shoppers. Their children learn when and how to touch merchandise and when to leave it alone.

Step Two

Teach your youngster that we should only touch things we can afford to pay for in case of an accident. This gives you something to say instead of, "Don't touch!" From this point on, it's probably more effective to say, "This costs $29. Can you afford to pay for it?"

Most children will say, "But I won't break it." The adult should then say, "That's not the point. We agreed that you can touch only those things you can afford to buy. Please put it back."

Step Three

Spend some time in the store actually practicing handling unbreakable items. Practice deciding which things should and should not be touched. Then spend a little time practicing the right way to touch items and put them back.

Step Four

Now it's time to catch the child doing things right so you can provide positive reinforcement: "Look how well you're doing! It makes me happy to see you act so grown up." If things aren't going well you can ask, "What was our agreement about that?"

Step Five

Once the lesson has been taught and there have been opportunities for practice, provide a short review before you go shopping again: "Tell me how you plan to handle your shopping today. I'm anxious to hear how well you can do."

Many battles with our children can be eliminated through these steps, which are designed to teach, practice, and reinforce. Our children are usually able to act in responsible yet independent ways. All we have to do is be willing to take some small risks to help them practice the art of becoming an adult.

Controlling our children is both impossible and undesirable.
Learn the real job of parenting in the next article.

What's a Parent For?

Volume 5, no. 4

"But how can I be a good parent if I can't make my kid do what I want him to do when I want him to do it?"

This bottom-line question finally helped us get to the root of the problem between two parents and their very rebellious 12-year-old. Our discussion didn't start with this question; it started with, "Your speech was very interesting, but what do you do with a child who never hears anything you say?"

I asked for more information. The mother said, "It's just like calling a cat. I call him to dinner, and he doesn't even flinch. It's like my words go in one ear and out the other."

"Let me give you an example. I'll walk up to him when he is playing with his computer and ask him to come to dinner. He just ignores me."

"What do you do then?" I asked.

"Well," she said, "I raise my voice, and he doesn't even pay attention then. It seems like I have to get really mad before he knows that I mean business."

"How does that work?" I asked.

"Well, he doesn't show any respect. He just starts in on me with complaints about our being on his back all the time. It ends up ruining dinner every night. What do you do?"

I suggested that some parents go to the child and calmly say, "We'll be serving dinner for the next 30 minutes. I sure hope you can make it, but if not, we'll be serving breakfast at the regular time."

"I could never do that," she said. "It's not good for him to miss a meal. He needs his nourishment!"

With this, I had some interesting thoughts run through my head about the quality of nourishment he gets when he is doing battle with his folks. I wondered whether we could ever find a documented case of a child suffering permanent damage from missing a meal.

When my mind came back to the present I asked, "Are you saying that this technique won't work, or are you saying that you just can't stand to think of him getting hungry during the night?"

With this she went on to tell me seven different reasons why she could not use the technique I had suggested. I could sense her becoming more stressed and anxious with each reason.

Then, with great exasperation, she blurted out, "But how can I be a good parent if I can't make him do what I want him to do when I want him to do it? Just tell me how to make him come to the table, eat his dinner, and show a little appreciation for a nice meal by not arguing with us all the time!"

Sad but true, I know of no one who can tell her how to do that. She is asking for control over something she can never control. It is impossible to control the thoughts and actions of another person. The very best we can do is to set up situations in which the other person either decides it is best to do as asked, or has the opportunity to find out that it might be in his/her best interest to do as asked by the parent.

It makes us wonder which is most important—to control how our children act and think, or to give them 18 years worth of experiences that show how the real world works. If we believe our job is to control our children, we will be inclined to operate like the mother in this story who demanded that her child come to dinner right now.

If we believe our job is to help children discover how the real world operates, and how to think for themselves, we will tend to act like the parent who says, "We will be serving dinner for the next 30 minutes. I sure hope you make it because we love eating with you."

6

Volume 6

When Parents Can't Agree on Raising Kids
Volume 6, no. 1

But what if I use the Love and Logic techniques and my spouse doesn't? Isn't that going to be a problem for the children?"

I often hear this question. I hear it from dads as often as from moms. Not to worry. Children adjust to the differences in adults almost instantly once they know their parents will back each other up. Parents with different parenting styles will not harm a child.

It becomes a problem only when one parent tries to change the other one. This can become serious when the child gets wind of it and begins pitting one parent against the other. It's called divide and conquer.

It's rare for two parents to be in total agreement when it comes to raising children. This is all part of a grand design whereby we usually marry or otherwise take on a partner who is strong in the areas in which we are weak. This usually works out well until we have children and discover our partner responds in a different way.

A typical scenario might go like this: Dad is a bit strict. Mom is a bit more lenient. Dad responds in a strict manner to two-year-old Festus, who immediately climbs up on Mom's lap for some sympathy.

Mom says to herself, "Wow, Dad is too strict. I better balance it out by being more gentle and lenient."

Dad sees this and says to himself, "Oh, oh! Look what a pushover Mom is. I'd better toughen up or this kid will get out of control." So he becomes even more strict.

Mom sees this and says to herself, "Oh, oh! Dad is getting way too strict. I'd better be more gentle yet or Festus will be ruined."

In many families, this begins a war of wills between two people who love each other. Several things may be taking place. Each parent may be digging in his or her heels. Either may be reluctant to admit fault. Perhaps they fear that the child may be damaged. It's easy to see parents can grow further and further apart in their beliefs about raising children.

Children sense this even when they don't hear their parents arguing about it. They begin to view the world of big people as a place where you are supposed to square off against each other. The bad news is that these children often square off against their parents and often use manipulation in order to drive a wedge between them. Worse yet, we find them manipulating teachers against teachers and parents against teachers at school.

The reason behind this behavior is that children learn how to be big only by imitating the big people in their lives. Sylvia Rimm once asked a youngster if he was more like his mom or more like his dad. He answered, "I'm more like my dad."

When asked why, he said, "When my mom asks him to do stuff, he doesn't do it. And when my teacher tells me to do stuff, I don't do it!" Up to this point, his mom and dad had been blaming the school for his lack of motivation.

Agree to disagree

It would be ideal if both parents agreed on a parenting style. But that is rare. If you don't agree, remember that your children will develop a special and different relationship with each of you.

In some families, unfortunately, the children develop a wonderful relationship with one parent but not the other. Remember that you can never be responsible for a relationship between two other people. Trying to be responsible for this just makes things worse for all involved.

Talk with your partner and agree that you'll each parent in your own way. Agree that you won't try to change each other. Agree that if one of you asks for advice, the other will relate what works for him or her. Agree that if one parent starts to work with a child, the other will stay out of it. Agree that you will never criticize each other's parenting techniques in front of the children.

Be prepared for complaints from your child about her treatment by the other parent. Many parents practice in advance so that their response is on the tip of their tongue. I suggest, "Well, Dad has his own ways. I hope you learn to work it out with him." Or, "Mom has her reasons for doing that. Maybe it would be helpful for you to talk to her about it."

Be a good model

The best way to get your partner to change is to give her or him permission not to change. Then become a good model. Use your Love and Logic parenting skills when the other can see the results. Wait for the time he or she asks how you make parenting look so easy! That's the time to share what you have learned.

In the next article, learn why "That's an option" is a powerful phrase.

"That's an Option"
Volume 6, no. 2

"Well, if you guys don't love me enough to give me more allowance, I'll just have to start selling drugs!"

"I guess that's one option," said Mom.

"That's an option? What do you mean that's an option!"

Mom shrugged and said, "That's one way to solve your problem."

"You've got to be crazy! What are you on?" questioned Mark.

"Nothing," replied Mom. "Even though I love you more than anything in the world, the time has come when you have to decide for yourself how you are going to live your life."

"No way! You're on something. Otherwise you'd be giving me a lot of grief about this! Do you know that I could get caught for dealing! I could go to jail!"

"Don't worry. Maybe you'll make enough money dealing to hire some good lawyers to get you some light time. I'm sure you've thought it all out. Anyway, just think. If you get caught the state will take care of you. You won't have to worry about allowance, room and board, or anything. Besides, some of those older men will just love to have you for a cellmate. They'll protect you from the other inmates."

"Wait a minute! How am I supposed to go to college?"

Mom laid back on the coach and said, "Oh you won't be in the slammer forever. With good behavior, you'll get out and go to college later. You might even be better prepared because you'll have had more life experiences."

"This is weird, man! Are you just going to sit there and let me ruin my life? Don't you even care about what happens to me? I can't listen to this! This is blowing my mind!" Then Mark stomped out of the room.

As farfetched as this sounds, it is an actual conversation between a Love and Logic parent and her son. This parent had learned how to keep the monkey on the child's back. She had learned that kids love to "hit" us like Mark did in this situation.

The child's whole idea is to get the parent into defending, advising, and demanding. Then the child goes into his or her judge role with statements like, "That's not fair," or "I can't do that." Before long, the parent totally owns a problem the child actually needs to learn to solve.

Analyzing this situation, we first see that the mother did not criticize Mark by saying, "That's stupid. Don't you dare do that!" She did not tell him what to do by saying, "If you want to go to the concert badly enough, you'll get out and get yourself an honest job." And Mom did not use anger, guilt, intimidation, or orders such as, "As long as you live in my house, you're not going to talk like that!"

This Love and Logic mother remembered that the response, "That's an option," will apply regardless of the stupidity of a child's suggestion. Kids are great at coming up with stupid options, such as:

"I'll just have to eat worms."
"I'll just have to quit school."
"I'll kill myself and then you'll be sorry."
"I'll just refuse to eat dinner."
"I'll run away and you'll never see me again."

Youngsters love these options because they usually get parents to do all the thinking and ultimately take over ownership of the problem.

However, "That's an option," will usually stop a youngster cold in his/her tracks, forcing some serious thought on his/her part.

The second skill Mom used was to present the advantages of selling drugs. She stated them in rather negative, yet enthusiastic terms. As you can tell from the dialog, it blew Mark's mind. He switched roles and began telling Mom what was wrong with dealing drugs.

Third, Mom knew that Mark could learn from this type of dialog because she had a reasonably good relationship with him and because things had gone well during the first eleven years of his life.

Later, this mother said to me, "You know, Jim, even if this approach hadn't worked so well, I still would have felt better trying it out than doing it the old way. Before, I would have been shocked, screamed at him about his stupidity, and ordered him to get his act together. I just know that he would have defied me either by dealing drugs or something else that would shock me even more."

"Besides, Jim, I had a lot of fun with this. The hardest part was keeping a straight face and trying not to laugh when he looked shocked."

The techniques our parents used just don't work anymore.
Learn why in the next article.

〜⌒

But It Worked for My Dad!
Volume 6, no. 3

"I don't understand this. It worked for my parents. When they told me to do something, I did it. But when I tell my kids to do something, they say they have rights. I can't understand why it worked for my parents, but it won't work for me!"

I hear this from frustrated parents almost every day. And it's not because they don't care or work hard to be good parents. It's just that the techniques our parents used so effectively won't work on today's children.

We learn to be parents by copying our own parents. This is actually the best way to learn anything. While this method worked for hundreds of years, suddenly our generation of parents has been caught in a bind.

As a result of the human rights movement, the world has changed—leaving our generation of parents as the first that can't do the job the way our parents did it.

What's changed? People discovered they had rights. Those behind the Iron Curtain even brought down their governments. And they did it without guns. The governments could no longer use the same old ways of controlling the people.

As the human rights movement becomes more prevalent in America, children seem to be more aware of their rights and have new beliefs about how they should be treated. Parents can no longer use the same old ways of controlling them. Children are bringing their parents to their knees every day without the use of guns.

On the other hand, my dad bossed me around all the time. Once, I mustered up enough nerve to say, "You can't talk to me like that. I've got rights."

He answered, "You'll have some rights when you grow up. In the meantime, you'll do as I say!"

I checked this out with my friends. "My daddy's mean! He yells at me and bosses me around," I told them.

"You're lucky," they said. "You've got a good dad, and that is what good dads do." I also found no support from teachers, newspapers, radio, or anywhere else. I decided that everyone must be right. I'd have to wait for my rights.

Now it's different. A youngster goes out into the neighborhood and complains, "My daddy's mean. He bosses me around!" Then someone says, "Call Social Services. You've got rights!"

There is considerable support for the idea that children's beliefs should be treated with respect and that youngsters should have choices about how they are treated. As a result, children don't respond well when they think adults are being unfair.

The following order is an example of an old technique: "George, pick up your toys and put them away now." If George lived years ago, he probably believed parents were supposed to talk that way and he would have been happy to do as ordered. He'd have said to himself, "My mom bosses me around because she loves me. She's a good mom, and I better do what she says."

Today's children don't say to themselves, "How fortunate I am to have a mom who loves me enough to boss me around." They think, "I'll show her that it doesn't work to order me around. I'll either not do it or do it in a way that drives her crazy. She can't talk to me like that."

A parent using one of the new techniques, such as those taught by the Love and Logic Institute, would not give this child a chance to be defiant.

This parent would say, "George, there's really no hurry to pick up your toys. Just have it done before your next meal. Now that might be tonight, tomorrow, or Saturday. When you have your next meal is really up to you.

So . . . you decide about when to pick up your toys and you also decide when your next meal will be. Good luck, Pal."

There are many different ways to apply the Love and Logic techniques. Another parent might handle the same problem by saying, "George, would you rather pick up your toys or have me do it? If you do it, the advantage is that you'll get to see your toys again."

"There's no hurry. If you have them picked up by dinner, I'll know you want to keep them. If I still see them out, I'll know you want me to pick them up. That way, you can be saying bye-bye to your toys while you eat dinner. It's really up to you. Good luck."

Of course, Love and Logic parents follow through and do just what they said they would. Their children quickly learn that their parents' word is as good as gold.

For better or worse, children learn by modeling their parents.
Jim discusses imitating in the next article.

☙

If We Could Only Raise Kids Instead of Mirrors
Volume 6, no. 4

For years, I have suggested that parents avoid telling their children how to solve their problems. Instead, I suggest asking if the youngster would like to hear what other kids have tried. Then, I suggest parents offer a menu of possibilities, ranging from the worst possible solution to best.

We then ask the youngster to look at the possible consequences of each choice before deciding on a course of action. This is a "no-lose situation." The child either makes a good choice and feels good about it or makes a bad one and gains wisdom through the experience of a poor choice.

These kinds of techniques usually make so much sense to parents that they rush home to try them out on the kids. Susan was no exception. It's obvious from the following dialog that she not only learned the new strategy, but used it well.

In fact, she was such a good model for the child that she found herself writing to me with one of those "what now" questions. She wrote that after she had tried out a new technique, her five-year-old said, "Gee, Mom, it looks like you've got a problem."

"Oh," Mom said.

"Your kids need more toys! They need more Cherry Merry Muffin Kitchen stuff."

"Oh," replied Mom.

"Would you like to know how other parents have handled this?"

"I guess so," said Mom.

"Some have bought more toys. Others just give the money to the kids. Let me know what you decide."

Then the child fell on the floor laughing. The letter ended with "Jim—now what?"

My advice would be to smile and say, "Nice try! You did that so well. I just know that you're going to be a great mommy someday." Then give the youngster a big hug and have some fun with the fact that she is learning by imitating.

Regardless of how we lead our lives, we raise children who are no more than mirrors of our own behavior. They imitate our actions, our tone of voice, our attitudes or values and even our fears. Copying is the way humans learn best.

I recently talked with a father who was upset with his teenage daughter, who had lied to her boss. She told him she was sick and then took off to spend the day with her boyfriend.

This dad was looking for an appropriate consequence when he came up with a painful insight. He said, "Do you suppose she picked that up from seeing me take a 'mental health day' from my teaching job? I've done that a number of times." And then he added, "It's sure painful to see your kids copying some of the things you're not proud of."

This insightful dad decided that instead of punishing his daughter he would talk to her about where she learned this behavior. He said he was going to tell her that he had been a poor example.

His parting words were,"I bet the two of us can come up with some ideas that will make both of us into better and happier people."

I'm proud of this man. He is a strong dad who can be a great example to all of us. While he is solving this problem, he is also modeling some effective problem-solving for his daughter. The nice thing about raising mirrors is that we can raise the kinds that make us feel proud when we look into them.

7

Volume 7

How to Boss Kids Around
Volume 7, no. 1

Many experts encourage us to replace orders and demands with choices. The odds go up that children will be more cooperative when they feel they have some control over their situation. This happens when they are offered choices.

It's hard to think of what choices to give when your children are giving you trouble. As one mother put it, the only choice she can think of at those times are, "Hey! Do you want to live or die!"

Needless to say, this is not an effective use of choices. She is in an emotional state which is not a good time to come up with choices.

There are also times when we have to either give orders or tell our kids there are no choices. The good news is that this won't be difficult if we are willing to set up a "savings account." This is done by giving them choices when everything is going well. Effective parents often give choices about things that don't make a lot of difference to them:

"Do you want to wear red socks or blue socks?"

"Do you want to wear your coat or carry it?"

"Do you want to eat what's on the table or wait for the next meal?"

"Do you want to go to your room with your feet touching the ground or not touching the ground?"

By offering children a lot of choices, we can then easily make a withdrawal from the savings account when we need to give orders.

I met a father who said, "Now I understand what my wife has been doing all these years. I always wondered about her routine with the kids at bedtime. She may be one of the world's greatest experts on creating a savings account of control. And you know what, Jim? She's never had a psychology course in her life!"

"You should hear how she talks with those kids and see how well it works":

Mom: "It's time to go to bed. Do you want to go now or when the TV show is over?"

Children: "When it's over."

Mom: (later) "OK, the program is over. Let's go to bed. Do you want a drink of water?"

Children: "Yeah! We need drinks."

Mom: "Do you want bathroom water or kitchen water?"

Children: "Kitchen water!"

Mom: "Good. You have to decide about things like that. Now, do you want it in a cup or a glass?"

Children: "In a glass."

Mom: "Good decision. Now, do you want a ride down to the bedroom or do you want to walk on your own?"

Children: "We want a ride!"

Mom: "Great. It's your choice. Now decide whether you want the light on or off, and whether you want to listen to music or have it quiet in here. Also, do you want the door shut or open?"

Children: "But we don't want to go to bed!"

At this time Mom makes a withdrawal from her savings account:

Mom: "Wait a minute. Didn't you just get to make a whole lot of choices? Don't I get a turn? Well, it's my turn to decide. Thanks for understanding. I'll see you in the morning."

Children: "I guess so."

There are times when we must boss our children around. The parents who do this with a minimum of rebellion are usually the ones who have set the groundwork by regularly giving their children choices when life is going well.

Children who don't have to fight regularly for their share of control are less likely to fight for it when we occasionally need to boss them around. Those who feel they have very little control will fight for control all the time! Which child would you most like to have living in your home?

Just because you accept your teen's activities
doesn't mean you approve of them.
Learn the difference in the following article.

↵

Don't Confuse Acceptance With Approval
Volume 7, no. 2

Parents and teens often find themselves in the heat of battle over extracurricular activities. Parents frequently confuse acceptance of these activities with approval of them. But there is a big difference. For instance, we can accept the fact that there are wars. That doesn't mean we have to approve of them. But it does mean we can listen to a discussion about war without being afraid that we are giving the impression we approve of war.

We hope our teens will discuss many of the things that take place in their lives. Like adults, teens make mistakes or can find themselves in difficult situations. It's helpful for them to be able to talk with an interested, not blaming, adult about these experiences.

The fact that they are willing to talk to us is a good sign. It gives them a chance to relive, in a safe way, what happened and get their own beliefs in order. Effective parents listen without being afraid that their willingness to listen means approval.

A parent who listens with interest and curiosity and asks sincere questions about the teen's thoughts, opinions, or values can actually help the youngster view his or her situation in a healthy way. Parents who use this approach find that the more they listen, the more their teens begin to evaluate the wisdom of the activity.

Wise parents are more concerned about their teen's plans for handling undesirable activities than they are about restricting those activities. Whether an activity is good or bad is not nearly as important as knowing your teen can handle the temptations associated with the activity. The following scenario illustrates this:

Teen: "Mom, I'm old enough to go to that concert. Can I go?"

Mom: "I'll know you're old enough when you can tell me about the possible pressures you're going to face and your plan for handling them."

Teen: "Gee, Mom. Are you worried I'm going to do drugs?"

Mom: "That's not what I said. I want to know what you are going to say when the other kids tell you that everyone does drugs at a concert, and when they say that you're not going to get hooked if you do them once in a while."

Teen: "Gee, Mom. Don't you trust me?"

Mom: "That's not the point. I know how hard it is to be in awkward situations. I also know that once you have thought it out and come up with a plan for handling those situations, you'll be ready to take care of yourself. I'll be glad to let you go to the concert when you can describe that plan to me."

This mother knows that the day this teen can describe her plan for handling these temptations and situations is the day she is ready for the activity and that Mom no longer needs to worry.

Acceptance of extracurricular activities is not the same as approval. Wise parents accept the activity and help their teens learn to handle the temptations associated with that activity.

In the next article, Jim shows how constant criticism leads children to a sad life.

Spirit Killers
Volume 7, no. 3

I know a man who met a killer. It was himself. He had systematically killed the spirit of the person he loved the most. He had killed the spirit of his own son.

What hurt this man the most was that he had done it out of his love and a desire for his son to grow up without the flaws he saw in himself. He discovered that he had killed his son's spirit, not on purpose, but with love and criticism.

Years later, this dad can't go back and change what he did. His grown son is seeing a therapist to try to rebuild his shattered self-confidence and discover happiness. Sadly, he has become the same kind of critic as his father.

Children who live with criticism grow up to be critical and chronically unhappy. Isn't this ironic? Many parents who criticize their children do so in an attempt to help them grow up without flaws. When asked what they want most for their youngsters, they say they want them to be happy adults.

It's also interesting that parents who are critical never admit to it. One extremely critical parent once said to me, "No! I don't criticize my daughter. I guide her! She must know what she's doing wrong so she doesn't continue to make the same mistakes."

If you could spy into this home, you would hear Mom's constant scolding about how her daughter washes her face, puts on a blouse that does not match and talks too loudly during breakfast. She even criticizes the quality of the child's kiss as she leaves for school.

"Is that any way to give your mother a kiss?"

Her daughter, still trying to measure up, comes back and tries again. "I'm sorry, Mom. I love you."

"I know you do," answers Mom. "I love you too. Now hold your shoulders back when you walk. People will think you don't have any pride!"

She humiliates her daughter in front of her friends with reprimands: "Now look at your friends when they talk to you. You'll never have any friends if you act like that!"

I once heard her yell out the front door to her daughter who was playing with her friends: "Your computer disks are all over the floor! Those disks are expensive! Maybe if you had to pay for them you'd be a little more careful!" She then marched the humiliated child into the house.

Mom describes this approach as guidance. But professionals have different terms for it—attacking, nagging, humiliation, fault-finding, ridicule, rejection, and criticism.

Regardless of the terms used to describe this style of parenting, the results are the same. They are deadly. They don't show up for years. Over time, these children become less and less confident. Their spirits slowly erode away. They even become their own best critics.

I have a friend who grew up this way. He has never found true happiness. He avoids trying things that appeal to him because he fears failure. Even though the person who severely criticized him in his youth is no longer alive, the voices are still in his mind.

"It's no longer my dad who does the criticizing," he says. "I've taken over that job myself. I constantly remind myself of my inadequacies. I spend much more time paying attention to what I do wrong than what I do right. I just hate it!

"But each year the problem gets worse. The more I recognize my faults, the more I have to be unhappy about."

This man has another regret: "The sad part is that I find myself criticizing my own children the same way my dad ragged on me. The more unhappy I am, the more I try to correct my children so they don't grow up to be like me. It's become a vicious circle."

Do yourself a favor. Do your children a favor. Remember that youngsters don't learn by being corrected. They learn through modeling and example.

Try to see your children as children, not small adults. They learn by making mistakes when we allow them to experience the consequences of those mistakes. Show empathy, not anger, as your children live with these consequences. Bite your tongue when you want to tell them what they did wrong. They can figure that out for themselves. Bite your tongue when you have impatient words that indicate your child does not measure up.

Instead, focus on what your children do well. Call these things to their attention ten times as often as you talk about what they don't do well.

You'll be rewarded with children who treat you well, notice your strengths instead of your faults, and who grow up to be happier adults who have broken the criticism cycle.

Is your child strong-willed?
Find out how to end the power struggles on the next page.

Strong-willed Children Can Be Their Own Best Teachers
Volume 7, no. 4

Bonnie was a strong-willed child who often fought with her mother. Then Mom started listening to some Love and Logic tapes. "These techniques are just what I need to handle my strong-willed daughter," Mom said after a short time.

Through the Love and Logic tapes, Mom learned some new ways to sidestep Bonnie's power struggles. Before long she was saying, "Parenting is fun again!"

Bonnie was a kindergartner. One fateful day, she forgot her permission slip for the class field trip. She found herself in the principal's office, where the principal was considering calling Bonnie's mother to obtain verbal permission.

Just then, a teacher came into the office. "Bonnie's mother is familiar with the Love and Logic principles," she said. "You know what Jim and Foster teach about responsibility. I don't think I'd call her if I were you. I'm sure her mother will give you all the support you need to allow Bonnie to live with the consequences of her mistake, as long as you do it with empathy instead of anger."

This put the principal in quite a bind. She herself is a recovering "helicopter" parent. She once demanded that her husband leave an important business meeting to take lunch money to their son! She said to him, "You have to do it. He's going to be hungry. After all, he's only 24 years old and it's his very first day at this job!"

You can imagine how difficult it was for her to tell Bonnie that she couldn't go on the field trip. However, the principal finally decided that she was more afraid of angering Bonnie's mother than she was of facing this kindergartner.

Mustering all her strength, she said, "Oh, Bonnie, this is so sad. The trips are always more fun when everyone goes. But, I'll tell you what we'll do. As soon as we get back, we'll tell you all about the trip."

No, Bonnie didn't take this lying down. She was burned! She went home and laid down the law to her Mom: "You can't let them to do that to me! You get over to the school and tell them they can't be mean to little kids just because they forgot their field-trip slip."

Mom had learned through Love and Logic that real-world lessons are remembered longer when the adult is sad and understanding instead of angry. Mom summoned her courage and said, "Oh, Bonnie, this is so sad. I bet it was a terrible day for you."

Then Mom then went to her bedroom to cry. She realized that when your child learns about the real world in real-world ways, it hurts you ten times more than it does the child.

Two weeks passed. One day when Bonnie returned home from school, Mom could see her knuckles were white from clutching a piece of paper. Bonnie was yelling. "Here, Mom. Sign this. I'm not going to miss this trip! I'm putting this permission slip in my backpack right now!"

Mom tells us she had to pry Bonnie's little fingers apart so she could take the permission form. She said, "Jim, do you know how hard it is to sign a soggy permission slip that's been in a kid's hot little hand for two hours? It's especially hard when the child is demanding 'You have to sign it right now! We can't wait for it to dry. You might forget. Do it now. Please!'"

The moral of this story comes in the form of a question. Who taught Bonnie to get that paper signed right away? Who taught her to put it in her backpack so she wouldn't forget it? Was it the teacher? Was it the principal? Was it her mother? Or was it Bonnie?

We can happily say that Bonnie is now learning to be more responsible. We are also pleased to report that she and her mother are not fighting as much anymore.

Mom has learned the secret. Children need opportunities to make mistakes. They need to be allowed to live with the consequences of those mistakes. They are fortunate when they have parents who offer genuine sadness and understanding while they experience those consequences.

Children have wonderful minds. They are capable of learning much more than most of us think. One of the most difficult parenting jobs is staying out of the way long enough for our children to figure things out for themselves. This takes both faith and support.

All of us have days when we need more support than others, especially those of us who are raising strong-willed children. Those are the days when you turn on your Love and Logic tapes and let Foster and me send you some strength and encouragement.

Remember that strong-willed children can grow into strong adults. This happens as long as they are allowed to make many decisions and then live with their decisions, instead of engaging their parents in battles over power. Review your tapes—*The Science of Control* and *Setting Limits for Kids*—for extra support when you find yourself getting hooked into these power struggles.

8

Volume 8

Children's Rooms
Volume 8, no. 1

Is your child's room a constant source of irritation and frustration? If so, join the ranks of parents throughout the country who are looking for answers to the messy room problem.

Years ago, I remember being so frustrated by this problem that I consulted Dr. Foster Cline, who later became my partner. He made some interesting points. "Jim," he said, "you have to realize that most kids keep their rooms the same way their parents keep their garages. Kids look at their rooms more like storage areas than showplaces."

He reminded me that when adults stay in a motel room for a few days, the room starts to look just like a kid's room. "It's that old problem of having too little room for the amount of stuff we like to have," he explained.

He also told me that studies do not support any connection between how children keep their rooms and how they eventually keep their homes. However, there appears to be a connection between how parents keep their parts of the house and how children take care of their homes when they grow up.

His advice? Foster suggested I "loosen up" about demanding perfect rooms and spend more time being a good model by picking up after myself. I didn't want to hear this. What I wanted to hear was a way I could continue to be messy while demanding that my kids be neat. He assured me I was expecting a miracle if I thought my kids were going to outperform me.

Show the kids how to be reasonable

We tried to be a little more understanding about the condition of our children's rooms. "We want to be reasonable," we said. "We'll back off and let you decide how you want to have your room as long as you don't trash out our parts of the house."

Then we made one more request: "Could you just shut your doors when we have company?"

The rooms didn't get a lot cleaner, but we had fewer arguments and power struggles. And, we were no longer embarrassed when company came. That improvement was certainly worth what we paid for it. We found that as we became more reasonable, our kids became more reasonable.

This gave us more power. We could then go to our children and say, "Aren't we usually pretty reasonable? Don't we usually let you have your rooms the way you want them? Well, could you be reasonable by cleaning them up now, just for us?" Wow! The kids actually agreed to help out!

Agree upon reasonable deadlines instead of "Do it now!"

The next step in our learning process was the discovery that you get a lot more cooperation from your children if you don't demand that they do things immediately.

It's much better to provide a reasonable deadline: "Would it be reasonable for you to have your rooms cleaned up by Saturday?" This gave us some time to figure out what we could do if they didn't comply. We even learned to say, "Everyone who has a clean room by Saturday at 9 a.m. will be going skating with us." As soon as they discovered we meant business, life became even easier.

Help them customize their rooms

Things really improved when we discovered that it paid to let our kids decide how they wanted their rooms to look. The more they became involved in picking paint colors and furniture, the more pride they took. Their interest improved the day we said, "These are your rooms. Mom and I think you are old enough to decide how you want them to look. Why don't you think about it. On Saturday, we'll go to the paint store and you can pick the colors you want." You'd be surprised how much pride they took in slapping the paint on the walls.

Later we said, "Why don't we all go to the furniture store and see what's there for kid's rooms? We're not going to buy anything right away, but it will give you a chance to start dreaming and planning. It will also give us a chance to start thinking about how much we can afford."

We had a great time, except that the kid's dreams and our budget didn't match. Instead of saying, "You don't need anything that expensive," we said, "Dad and I will try to figure out how much we can afford and you can start finding a way to earn or make up the difference."

Since then, we've learned that "matching funds" are a great way to teach responsibility. It's amazing how much better kids take care of the items they have worked for and earned. We even discovered that it was helpful to keep a list of household jobs that we were willing to pay for on the refrigerator. The kids could go to that list anytime they were looking for a job. We made sure these weren't their regular chores, but jobs that we ourselves didn't like to do. It's surprising what kind of work youngsters will do when they want money badly enough.

We once dreamed of neat, tidy rooms. But now our dreams are different. The kids are grown and gone now. We miss them terribly. The rooms are neat as a pin because our kids are no longer here to trash them. We no longer have posters all over the walls and ceilings. There are no toys, car parts, or clothes lying around. The rooms need to be cleaned only occasionally. They are just the way we once dreamed they should be.

The only trouble is that we would gladly exchange the neat, orderly rooms for the messy ones we used to see every day if we could just have the kids back in the house. While they lived here, we dreamed of neat tidy rooms. Now that they're gone, we dream of messy ones. The world just isn't fair.

Jim discusses the difficult issue of grade retention in the next article.

Does Repeating a Grade Ever Work?
Volume 8, no. 2

"My son's teacher says he needs to repeat his grade next year. I just don't know about that. How do I know for sure if that's the best thing to do? I want him to do well in school, but this has to be a terrible blow to his self-confidence. It's hard enough to keep him thinking positively about school. What do I do?"

I hear this question over and over again from parents each spring. The question is an expression of frustration and anger over the fact that their children's achievement problems haven't been solved. It's a time of shattered dreams. It's also a time for some very serious decision-making by both school personnel and parents on the possibility of retaining a child.

The fallout from this decision will have a lasting impact on a child. It should therefore not be made lightly. We have seen some lives changed for the better in cases where children have been appropriately retained. However, these cases are in the minority. Research indicates that most retentions leave scars that are difficult to heal.

Many students who are candidates for retention have either failed or refused to turn in written assignments. It is important to note that uncompleted written assignments are not proof that a child is not learning.

I have seen many children score high on achievement tests at the end of the year even though they have a history of uncompleted assignments. This, of course, is a major frustration for teachers.

Punishment is tempting

Teachers and parents are sometimes tempted to show the child that he/she is not going to get away with being an underachiever. Retention and/or threats of retention are often the first things that come to mind. If we buy into this way of thinking, it means we believe the child has all the abilities and skills needed to be successful; the child has no self-concept problems; the child is not dealing with any emotional issues; and the child just wants to be unsuccessful in school and in life.

I wish it were that simple. If so, all we'd have to do is occasionally threaten children with retention. Good grades would immediately follow.

The root causes of underachievement in school are not easily discovered. They hide deep within the subconscious minds of children. Professionals recently discovered that 97 percent of children who avoid their schoolwork have problems related to self-concept or self-concept problems with emotional overlays. These kids are not part of "organized crime," but are often damaged, discouraged, or disenchanted with the possibility of success at school.

When to retain?

1. Identify the root causes

Until the root causes of a child's academic problems are found, retention will not only be a waste, it may be permanently damaging. *The Underachievement Syndrome* by Sylvia Rimm, is an excellent source to help parents and teachers work together in determining the causes of a child's underachievement.

Identifying the causes behind the problem cannot be accomplished by either parent or teacher alone. They must work together to look at both family patterns and the reactions of the child at school.

Caution! Do not consider retention until this first step has been completed.

2. Create a plan for success

Retention will also be a waste and permanently damaging unless a solid plan with a 90 to 100 percent chance of success is developed.

This plan, created after the root causes are identified, usually addresses changes in family patterns; strong cooperation between parents and teachers; individual counseling for the child, and different teaching and relationship strategies at school. Retention should not be considered until this step has been completed.

People often say, "Let's retain this child. I just think he/she could benefit from another year of maturity." This thinking looks at only one aspect of the problem and does not guarantee that the root causes have been considered. Nor does it indicate there is any plan of action that might lead to success.

3. Administer "Light's Retention Scale"

H. Wayne Light, Ph.D., believes that there are 19 aspects of a child's life that should be considered before deciding to use retention. He has developed a scale that is very useful to parents and professionals who are considering retention for a child.

Light's scale considers age, sex, knowledge of the English language, physical size, present grade placement, previous retention, brothers and sisters, parents' school participation, life experiences, family moves, school attendance, intelligence, history of learning disabilities, present level of academic achievement, attitude about possible retention, interest in school work, immature behavior, emotional problems, and history of serious behavior problems.

Needless to say, Dr. Light warns us there is much to be considered before making the crucial decision to retain. Information about this scale is available from Academic Therapy Publications, 20 Commercial Boulevard, Novato, CA 94947.

4. Provide effective counseling

It is important that child, parent, and teacher each feel good about the retention. If any one of them does not, it is doomed. It is especially important for youngsters to feel good about the decision. Children who are not adequately and effectively counseled on retention usually suffer long-term self-concept problems, which result in additional learning problems as the years go by.

Children must frequently hear and sincerely believe that their parents will continue to love them regardless of their success in school.

Questions to ask

Retention is rarely a solution for underachievement problems. It is effective only when all of the following questions can be answered with a resounding YES:

1. Have all the root causes of the problem been discovered?

2. Has an effective treatment plan been developed and accepted by both the professionals and parents?

3. Does Light's Retention Scale indicate the child is a good candidate for retention?

4. Does the student feel good about the retention?

5. Do the parents feel good about the retention?

6. Does the school feel good about the retention?

If any one of these questions receives a negative answer, forget about retention until all six questions receive a resounding YES.

In the next article, Jim describes a potential tragedy that becomes a positive learning experience.

Turning Bad Decisions Into Wisdom
Volume 8, no. 3

The beauty and strength of Love and Logic, I am often told, is that once a person understands the basic principles, he/she can apply them to new and different situations. In other words, we can solo!

There are many different ways to help our children carry the lion's share of thinking. There are many different ways to force decision-making. And, there are many unique and creative ways to express genuine sadness for children who make mistakes.

A father recently reminded me of the value of using childhood mistakes as opportunities to gain wisdom and experience. He related the following opportunity his 15-year-old son provided:

Dad received a call from the police station notifying him that his son had been picked up for shoplifting. A million thoughts went through this father's mind as he drove to pick up his son. They included the old way he would have handled the situation before his Love and Logic training.

In the past, he would have ranted and raved and rescued. But this time, he would use empathy to drive home the pain of this lesson. He remembered what his Love and Logic training had said about these situations: "Let the consequence be the bad guy and the parent be the good guy."

Dad met a very sheepish child at the detention center. "Don't be mad, Dad. I'm sorry. I'll never do anything this stupid again!"

"I'm not mad, Son, but I really feel sorry for what you're going to have to face. I guess you know that you'll have to appear in court. Who knows what the judge will do. I hope you're strong enough for this. I have no way of knowing what will happen."

Dad went on to explain that no one should ever appear before a judge without legal representation. Then he said to his son, "I'll make a deal with you. I'll never ask you to pay for a lawyer for me. On the other hand, I won't pay for your lawyer. So I suggest you call around to some law offices and find out how much you're going to have to pay to be represented in court."

Needless to say, this was a bit of a shock for the 15-year-old child. However, he mustered up his courage and made several calls. Later, in a state of depression, he said to his dad, "Do you know that the cheapest lawyer I could find wants to charge me $600? That's a rip-off!"

"It's never cheap to hire professional help," said Dad. "Maybe I can help. In this state, parents can represent their children in court. I don't have a license to practice law, so I wouldn't want to charge as much as a lawyer. If you want, I'll do it for half price. But maybe you want to think about that for a while. Let me know."

The youngster thought for a moment and then said, "I guess I better have you represent me. But I don't even have $300. If you do it, will you loan me the money?"

Dad agreed to loan him the money, but the boy was in for more big surprises. Dad took him to the office supply store where he purchased a legal promissory note form. The two of them then sat down together and filled out the form. The son signed the document.

"Now we'll need to take a trip down to the Secretary of State's office," said Dad. "Any time you loan money, there needs to be a legal paper trail in case the person who borrows the money fails to honor the contract and you have to repossess the collateral."

Father and son finally appeared before the judge of the juvenile court. "Young man, are you represented by counsel?" asked the judge.

"Yes sir. My dad's not a lawyer, but he agreed to do it for half price. He even loaned me the money and made me put up collateral and sign a note. And, he made me go with him to file it with the Secretary of State and all that stuff."

"How do you plead in this matter?" asked the judge.

"My client pleads guilty, Your Honor," said Dad.

"Fine," answered the judge. "Do you have anything to say before I rule?"

"Yes, Your Honor," offered Dad. "This is a good boy. He's never been in trouble before. He does his chores and works hard at school. He admits that he made a big mistake and does not plan to repeat this behavior. He is requesting that you consider a deferred judgment. He is even suggesting that the deferred judgment be 12 months instead of the regular six months so he can prove to the court that he can stay out of trouble for that period of time."

The judge struck his gavel. "So ordered. Stay out of trouble young man. Now stand down!"

Father and son left the courtroom together. They were silent as they walked to their car. As they settled into their seats for the trip home, the boy looked at this dad and said, "You know what, Dad? You were awesome in there!"

I think we would all agree that this potential tragedy was turned into a great learning opportunity. And I bet we'd all agree that we know about a young boy who has a lot more respect and love for his dad. Would that we could all be so fortunate.

Use the one-liners, presented in the next article,
to avoid getting hooked into arguments with your children.

Love and Logic "One-liners"
Volume 8, no. 4

Kids seem to have a repertoire of "hooks" they use to get their parents to argue with them. Here are some responses designed to get parents off the hook and cause their children to do some heavy-duty thinking.

The majority of these Love and Logic "One-Liners" are most effective when said with genuine compassion and understanding. Holding the child's hand or placing your hand gently on the child's shoulder greatly increases the effectiveness of each response.

Practice delivering just one of the following responses. You'll know when you're ready to use the one-liner when you find yourself thinking, "Come on, kid. Make my day! I can't wait to try out my new skills!"

Child: "IT'S NOT FAIR!"

Parent: (Optional responses)
"Probably so."
"Could be."
"True."
"That's a possibility."
"I'm afraid so."

Use these same parental responses for the following childhood complaints:

"That's stupid!"
"My friends don't have to do that!"
"This sucks!"
"I don't care!"
"All the other kids get to . . ."

Child: "YOU'RE JUST USING THAT LOVE AND LOGIC STUFF AGAIN!"

Parent: "Thanks for noticing. I'm trying to be a better parent."

Child: "WHERE'S THAT NICE MOTHER I USED TO HAVE?"

Parent: (Optional responses)
"Gone forever, I'm afraid."
"Who knows?"

"Would you rather I went back to yelling and screaming?"
"What was my old way? I've forgotten."

~

Child: "I HATE YOU!"

Parent: (Optional responses)
   "That's sad. But I still love you."
   "Do you think you'll hate me forever, or do you think you'll
    get over it?"
   "I guess I'm kind of hard to love at times."
   "Do you think you'll still hate me at dinner time?"

~

Child: "YOU DON'T LOVE ME!"

Parent: "Nice try." (Say this with a smile on your face and lilt in your
   voice.)

~

Child: "EVERYBODY ELSE GETS TO DO IT!"

Parent: "What do you think I think about that?"

~

Child: "I'M NOT DOING IT, AND YOU CAN'T MAKE ME!"

Parent: (Optional response)
   "Don't worry about it now."
   "There's no hurry. Just have it done before your next meal.
    That could be today, tomorrow, or Saturday. It's really up to
    you."
   "Take your time. I only expect it done by the end of the day."

~

Child: "WHY DO I HAVE TO?"

Parent: "If you don't understand why after you finish, I'll be glad to
   explain."

~

Child: "I'M THE ONLY ONE WHO EVER HAS TO."

Parent: "I bet it feels that way."

↩

Child: "BUT I DON'T NEED MY COAT!"

Parent: "Won't it be exciting to find out."

↩

Child: "BUT I DON'T LIKE THIS KIND OF FOOD!"

Parent: (Optional responses)
"All the more for the rest of us."
"Maybe you'll like what we have for the next meal better."
"That's up to you."

↩

Child: "IT'S NOT MY FAULT. THE TEACHER JUST DOESN'T LIKE ME!"

Parent: (Optional responses)
"It must feel awful to get grades like that. Is there any way I can help?"
"I know how bad grades hurt, but we'll love you regardless of the number of years it takes you to get through that grade."

↩

Child: "YOU'RE SO OLD-FASHIONED!"

Parent: (Optional responses)
"Thanks for noticing."
"I bet that's true."
"Old-fashioned parents must be a drag for you."
"Be sure to smile when you say that."
"Antiques are rare and priceless."

↩

Child: "DON'T TRY TO PULL THAT LOVE AND LOGIC STUFF ON ME!"

Parent: "Oh really. What kind of stuff do you want me to pull on you?"

Child: "WE DON'T HAVE HOMEWORK. THE TEACHER LETS US DO IT ALL AT SCHOOL."

Parent: (Optional responses)
"Nice try. Bring me a note from your teacher."
"I'm sure your report card will tell the story on that. Good luck."
"Oh, honey. Do I look like I believe that?"
"Do I look like I just fell off the Stupid Mom truck?"
"I might have a hard time believing that if I said it myself."

Child: "I REALLY NEED THOSE $125 RUNNING SHOES!"

Parent: "Go for it! I'll donate $35. When you earn the rest, you'll have them. I can't wait to see you wearing them!"

Child: "IF YOU LOVED ME, YOU'D LET ME . . ."

Parent: "Nice try."

Child: "YOU NEVER . . ." or "YOU ALWAYS . . ."

Parent: "I bet it looks that way. Tell me more."

Child: NO WORDS BUT THE "ROLLING EYES" SYNDROME.

Parent: The best response is no response, but if you must say something, try this:
"What are the eyes saying today, Pal?"

Child: "I DON'T HAVE TO PUT UP WITH THIS. I'M GOING TO LIVE
         WITH DAD!"

Parent: "I love you wherever you live."

⌐

Reminder: These responses are never intended to be flippant remarks that discount the child's feelings. They absolutely must be said with compassion and understanding. If an adult uses these responses to try to get the better of a child, the problem will only become worse. The adult's own attitude at these times is crucial to success.

9

Volume 9

Get the "Right Now" Monkey Off Your Back
Volume 9, no. 1

Have you ever had that shocked reaction to something your child did? I'm referring to that helpless feeling when you think, "Oh, no! I just don't know what to do." This is even more frustrating since most of us grew up believing parents must react immediately so the child will learn from the experience.

Not to worry. Help is on the way. Love and Logic parents know they don't need to have all the answers on the spot. They have learned that it is even more effective to delay dealing with a problem as long as the youngster knows something is going to happen.

Consider a situation in which your 16-year-old daughter has gone out for the evening. She said she would be home by 11:30. It is now 2:14 in the morning and she is still nowhere to be seen. My guess is that you have been worrying and pacing since 11:30. Eventually your worry turns to anger.

At 2:15 A.M., your daughter walks through the front door. Is she going to hear all about your undying love for her or is she going to hear, "Where have you been? I've been worried sick! You could have been hurt somewhere for all I knew. Don't you ever pull that stunt again. You're grounded!"

Why do parents react this way? There are probably several reasons. We want the child to know how important the situation is. We also want the youngster to own this problem and be motivated to behave better the next time. However, have you ever seen this kind of parental reaction create a lasting change of behavior on the part of the child?

Consider this alternative reaction by a worried parent. As her daughter comes home she is met with, "Oh, Nancy. I'm so glad you're OK. I've been worried sick about you. Give me a hug and go to bed. We'll deal with this later after I've figured out what to do. Don't worry about it tonight."

Needless to say, you are going to have a very shocked teenager. She is also not going to be able to argue since she doesn't yet know what to argue about. We also know that she will not be able to dismiss this easily from her mind as she tries to go to sleep.

You have now freed yourself to "gang up" on her in the morning. You can seek out help and advice from any number of sources. You can talk with friends, a counselor, a teacher, etc., to help arrive at a consequence that will make sense to your daughter.

Another benefit is that you can deliver the consequence when you are well prepared and calm. You could wait until Friday when Nancy announces she wants to go out. "Oh, Nancy, I just don't think I'm strong enough to worry about you tonight. Stay home, please."

Of course, Nancy is not going to accept this graciously. This is a shock. She thought she'd gotten away with coming in late the other night. We can expect her to be upset and quick to use her "brain drain" techniques: "Mom! That's not fair!"

At this point Love and Logic parents switch into their "one-liner" mode. Remember that it is the job of the youngster to do all the thinking while the parent simply replies with, "Probably so." The discussion probably will follow this pattern:

Nancy: "Making me stay home tonight is stupid!"

Parent: "Probably so."

Nancy: "But I promised my friends."

Parent: "I bet you did."

Nancy: "My friends are going to hate me for this."

Parent: "That's a possibility."

Nancy: "I hate you!"

Parent: "Nice try, Nancy."

This teenager might become as angry as the one who called the Love and Logic Institute one January, screaming, "Jim Fay has got to be stopped! Everything was just fine at our house until my parents went to listen to him. Now they go around the house with these silly little smirks on their faces. And all they can say is stupid things like, "Probably so," and "Nice try." She added, "My parents are driving me nuts!"

It's true. Youngsters who find themselves demoted from head of the household to child have a tough adjustment period. But they get over it and are eventually much happier, more responsible, and fun to be around.

As you think about these two different ways of dealing with a child, it's easy to see that delaying the consequence is much more effective. It gives you time to think, enlist some help, and deal with the child when both of you are calm.

A Love and Logic pearl

Whenever possible, deal with a situation when the problem is not taking place. Learn to say, "I'm not sure what to do about this. I'll get back to you."

Of course, it is best to remember that some situations don't lend themselves to this approach. Don't abandon common sense. Delaying action is never a good idea when a child is playing with a loaded revolver or running out into traffic. However, delayed consequences can be very helpful when we are facing certain problems:

The teen has wrecked the family car

Parental response: "I'm so sorry that happened. I'm not sure what I'm going to do. I'll get back to you on that. But I'm sure you'll drive again someday when you have paid off all the damages."

Child caught shoplifting

Parental response: "This is so sad for you. I'll have to get back to you after I've thought this through. In the meantime, I'll just have to wish you good luck with Juvenile Court."

Child suspended from school

Parental response: "Wow! What a problem for you. I'm not sure what I'm going to do, but I'll let you know after I've thought this over. You might want to be thinking of a way to get yourself back in favor with the principal."

Child has stolen money from the parent

Parental response: "Right now I'm pretty mad. Maybe it's best if I wait to talk with you later. I'll let you know in a few days what I'm going to do. You probably have a repayment plan in mind."

Child loses Dad's tools

Parental response: "As soon as I calm down, I'll spend some time thinking about what I'm going to do about this. What I do depends upon the kind of a solution you come up with. Good luck."

These are all unfortunate situations that can provide valuable lessons for children. Take time to think things out before dealing with them. None of them amounts to a crisis. By confusing them with a crisis, you'll be tempted to react on the spot and possibly lose the real teaching value of the child's mistake.

Learn how to give your child an "unfair" advantage in the next article.

How to Give Your Kids an Unfair Advantage
Volume 9, no. 2

Susie was an Asian child who was adopted by an American family that had solid values relating to achievement and personal responsibility. In a few short years she had moved to the head of her class.

Her classmates periodically asked her about how she got such high grades. They thought it was because Asians often excel at academics. She answered that she always did her homework before she went out to play.

Susie was named the class valedictorian and delivered the address at graduation. This caught the attention of many other children's parents. "Why is this?" they asked. "She lives in an Anglo family, but performs like an Asian."

One couple actually called Susie's parents in an attempt to gain insight. Susie's father mentioned that they shared some of the Asian values of hard work, struggle, and personal responsibility. He said Susie was expected to be responsible. When she was not, natural consequences were applied. He also related that they expected Susie to do her chores, be respectful of her parents, and apply herself to her schoolwork.

"Susie knows where we stand," said Dad. "She knows that in America she has the right to life, liberty, and the pursuit of happiness; not the right to life, liberty, and someone else to provide happiness for her. Susie is busy pursuing her own happiness through achievement and personal responsibility."

"Wait a minute!" replied the other parents. "Doesn't that give her an unfair advantage over the other children? Come on, Mr. Tyler. This is America. Whatever became of equal opportunity?"

"I guess if you look at it that way, there may never be equal opportunity. As long as some people work harder than others and place a high value upon achievement through struggle, they will always have an advantage over others. I guess that's the America I know."

Every time we hire new employees at the Love and Logic Institute, we are faced with the realization that some applicants have an unfair advantage over others. They are the ones who get the jobs.

We don't look at their school grades. Instead, we interview them extensively to determine their level of personal responsibility. Can they arrive at work on time? Do they take responsibility for their own actions? Do they pursue their own success or do they wait for others to hand it to them? Do they blame the system or others for their problems?

America's founding fathers dedicated our nation to life, liberty, and the pursuit of happiness. Americans knew they had a chance for success through struggle. As a result, struggle made America great.

But over the years, we have gradually tried to protect our children from struggle. Many parents now say, "I don't want my children to have to struggle like I did. I want them to have a better life and all the things I never did."

The results of this attitude are now being seen in our public schools as fewer and fewer children appear willing to accept struggle as a necessary part of learning. Teachers are working harder and harder to find new ways to motivate students. What makes it even more difficult is that students often believe teachers are being mean by asking them to struggle.

The schools are being criticized because kids are not achieving as well as they did in the past. However, changing the schools will not solve this problem. America will be plagued with underachieving students until our entire society changes its attitude and messages about the value of struggle. That's the bad news.

The good news is that your child can stand out and have a real advantage over others by learning to struggle and to be responsible early in life. When teachers challenge kids who have struggled, those kids think, "No big deal. I'm not afraid to struggle. In the end, I'll get what I want by struggling."

Give your child the advantage

CHORES

Learn how to get your children to do their chores without a battle. Regardless of what your kids say about chores, it's important that they learn to contribute to the welfare of the family. It's reasonable to expect children as young as six to do at least 20 minutes of chores each day.

Spend a couple of weeks listing all the jobs that have to be done for your family to survive. Keep this list on the refrigerator. Each time you think of another family job, add it to the list. This list should include all the jobs parents usually do, such as earning the money, keeping the checkbook, paying the bills, driving the car, shopping, cooking food, making beds, washing clothes, etc. Invite the children to list the things they need their parents to do for them.

Hold a family meeting to divide up the jobs. Have the kids select the jobs they would most like to do. In the event they don't like any of the jobs, have them choose the ones they hate the least. It's best to assign kids jobs they can complete individually. If they have to depend on each other, or if they do the chore together, you can expect unnecessary fights or arguments.

One technique for getting chores done is to say, "There is no hurry each day to do your chores. Just be sure they are done before the end of the day." Do not remind them about the chores.

If the jobs are not done by the end of the day, say nothing and let the kids go to bed. Let them sleep for 30 to 45 minutes and then wake them up. Remind them that the end of the day is near and they are to get up and finish their work. Don't take "no" for an answer.

If you are looking for additional tips on getting chores done, refer to the Love and Logic audio cassette titled *Chores*. It provides many different techniques.

MATCHING FUNDS

Kids are bombarded with media ads about material things. It's tempting to give them all you can as a show of love. This unconditional giving robs children of the opportunity to struggle and puts them at risk for underachievement in school.

It's also just as tempting to say, "You don't need those things." This is also not effective. Even in the rare event that a parent pulls this off, it robs the child of a chance to struggle.

Times when children ask you to buy something are opportunities to provide success through struggle. This is the time for the parent to implement "matching funds." For example, Tommy announces, "I really need those basketball shoes. All the other kids have them and they're only $125."

The wise parent responds with, "You ought to have them. I can't wait to see how you look in them. I'll contribute $35. As soon as you earn the rest, you'll have those shoes."

"But that's not fair. The other kids' parents buy them."

"I know. It's rough living the way we do. Let me know when you're ready for the $35."

Tommy will wear those new shoes with greater pride once he has struggled to earn them.

Use your personal value system to dictate the amount you provide each time. Sometimes you may contribute 75%, sometimes you will provide 10% and sometimes you might even contribute 90%. There is no firm rule for the way you choose to use your money. Also keep in mind that an occasional gift doesn't hurt a thing. Children who earn what they get gradually learn self-respect, resourcefulness, the value of money, and most importantly, that problems are solved through struggle.

NEVER GIVE JUST ONE SOLUTION

Children who solve their own problems have more self-respect than children who don't. It's very tempting to run interference for children. That's because it's hard on adults to see children having problems. However, children whose parents frequently solve their problems grow up to be emotional cripples. These children come to believe their parents' unstated message that they can't solve their own problems.

It appears natural for many kids to "drop the ball" when they have a problem. They look to their parents with pathetic voices: "I can't do it."

It's even more natural for parents to say, "Oh, no. If I don't pick up the ball, the child will never do it for himself." These parents soon find themselves sucked into their child's problem. The sad part is that most parents will tell you their kids never seem to like the parents' solutions anyway.

The next time your child comes to you with a problem, listen with empathy. Then follow with a question: "It sounds like that's really bothering you. What do you think you're going to do?"

Most kids will say, "I don't know."

Then you can say, "That's sad not to know. Would you like to hear what some other kids have tried?"

If the youngster says yes, tell the youngster you'll give it some thought and get back to him/her. This gives you a chance to think it out or to call a friend to help make up a list of both good and bad suggestions. There is no advantage to giving an immediate solution.

The importance of all this is to provide some choices for the child instead of just one solution. Present these solutions to the child one at a time. At the same time, require your child to evaluate each solution. For example: "Some kids get an army of kids to threaten the other kids. How do you think that would work out?"

I once watched a parent do this. In this case, the mother couldn't think of a good solution, so she gave four bad suggestions. Each time she asked, "How would that work?" Finally the youngster said, "Those ideas aren't any good. I think I'll just go try to talk it out with her." This mother remarked that it was great to see her daughter learn to think for herself.

DON'T PAY FOR GOOD GRADES OR PUNISH FOR BAD GRADES

I have often asked children who are not doing well in school this question: "Who do you think worries the most about your grades—you or your parents?" I always get the same answer: "My parents."

As long as children have others who worry about their problems, they don't worry about them. It's as if they're saying, "My parents have that worry well in hand. No sense in both of us worrying about it."

Parents who offer to pay for good grades or punish for bad ones are taking over too much of the worry about grades. This also raises the odds the child will see achievement as something that is being forced rather than offered.

Once a youngster sees grades as part of a power struggle, the issue is no longer the value of a good education, but who is going to win. As long as a child has two choices, to succeed or not to succeed, there is still a good chance for success. However, a child in a power struggle can see only one choice—winning the power struggle.

The One Year Plan is a tried-and-true approach to avoiding this power struggle while convincing youngsters that they own their grades and success. It takes us back to the good old days of the Bill of Rights—rights to life, liberty, and the pursuit of happiness instead of someone else pursuing happiness for you.

I offer the One Year Plan with a guarantee. Use it exactly the way it is outlined. If your child is not a better student at the end of one year, call me at (303) 278-7552 or toll-free at 1-800-338-4065. I will give you a free audio cassette album for proving me wrong.

This article first appeared in "The ABC's of Education in Metro Denver," a 1993 publication of Denver Relocation Resources.

If your grown children still live at home,
the next article will be of particular interest.

When It's Time for Them to "Get a Life"
Volume 9, no. 3

"What do I do? I'm at my wits' end! My grown son still lives at home. He doesn't respect our house rules. He never cleans up after himself. He lounges around and never lifts a finger to help.

"And worse yet, we can't seem to motivate him to get a job. He isn't even civil to us. When we try to tell him to treat us better and that he needs to get a job, he gets belligerent and tells us to get off his case."

You'd be amazed at how often I hear about these kinds of situations. When presented with this problem, I usually ask who is subsidizing this irresponsible son's easy lifestyle. Whose food is he eating? Whose car is he driving? Whose utilities is he using?

The answer is usually, "Well, ours, but . . . " This is often followed with a list of explanations, excuses, and reasons such as, "Well, he doesn't have the money to take care of himself," or "He's saving his money to buy a car."

Please tell me, readers. Would you put up with this for one minute if it were anyone but your own child sucking off your personal resources, while at the same time treating you with such disrespect? Of course not! You'd say, "Out! Get a life!" The answer is easy to see when it doesn't involve your own child.

A surefire way to cripple a person is to allow him/her to sponge off you. People who are warm, comfortable, protected, and well-fed usually have little motivation to change their lifestyles.

The way to motivate a person to get off the couch, look for a job, and become personally responsible is to take away his/her free ride. The way to teach a child how to take care of himself is by taking care of yourself. This means telling him/her you no longer can provide room and board.

This is scary for many parents, who say, "But that's so mean. He'll hate me if I make him move out, and I just feel so guilty asking him to pay room and board."

He will not hate you. In fact, normal humans hate to feel dependent upon others. Since this hate is so painful, it is usually transferred to the person who provides the support. Hostility/dependency take the form of angry, hostile and hateful behavior.

Many adult children who have been asked to leave the home are angry at first. They try using guilt on their parents. They often do their best to prove their parents made a big mistake.

Many of these youngsters appear to hit "rock bottom" in their desperate attempts to get their parents to allow them to return to the security of home. Some of them try rejection. They leave home and don't write or call for a long period of time.

The good news is that many eventually make overtures to come back into the relationship with the parents. And in most cases, they thank their parents for forcing them to grow up. I've heard many say to their parents: "Putting me out of the home was the best thing you ever did for me. Thanks for making a man out of me."

"But I can't just throw him out! What will he do?" is a typical reaction to my advice.

"What will he do?" is a question that helps us understand part of the problem. It's a good guess the son never has worried about what he will do. He subconsciously knows he won't have to be concerned about it. His parents have taken over that responsibility for him. It's not his problem. It's their problem.

The first step toward a solution is for the parent to believe, "If I don't concern myself with what he does, he'll have to take over that concern."

Then the parent can take on the more important role—that of teaching the child to take care of himself by demonstrating how it is done.

Solving the problem

When parents typically don't take care of themselves, and when their youngster is hostile or dependent, the stage is set for very difficult communication. This is not a good time to discuss the youngster leaving the nest.

I suggest it is better for the parents to provide the youngster with a "Good Neighbor Policy" letter. Putting their thoughts in writing raises the odds that the young man will receive his parents' entire line of thinking without feeling the need to become defensive or to start another argument.

The following is a letter that was used very effectively by some loving parents:

Dear Son,

We love you very much and want the best for you. So we are writing to you instead of talking with you in hopes that you will think about this for a few days before feeling the need to respond.

Our greatest dream for you is that you grow up to be independent, happy and able to take good care of yourself.

In our enthusiasm to make this happen, we have made some mistakes. We thought our lectures and criticism would help you, but they have only damaged our relationships with you. For that, we are genuinely sorry.

We didn't realize we would first have to take care of ourselves or you would never be able to see how it was done. We wish to apologize for this and admit that we have a lot of catching up to do if we are ever going to help you learn to take care of yourself.

The way we are going to do this is through what is known as the "Good Neighbor Policy." From now on, all of our decisions about you will be based upon this policy.

For example, if a good neighbor we loved dearly asked us for a loan, we would provide the money if the neighbor signed a promissory note and provided adequate collateral.

If a good neighbor came to us needing a place to stay, we would allow him/her to stay with us for a short time. We would provide room and board at a reduced rate, providing the neighbor paid in advance and was willing to live by our house rules. That way, he/she could continue to have both self-respect and independence.

As of the last day of this month you have the same opportunity. You may live here at the room-and-board rate of $400 per month—payable in advance on the first day of the month—if you are willing to live by our house rules. Or, you have the option of living elsewhere by your own house rules.

If you choose to live elsewhere and are kind enough to let us visit you from time to time, we agree to live by your house rules while in your home.

We know this is a difficult decision. We know that sometimes sons have difficulty telling their parents it is time for them to be on their own.

In the event you can't decide, we will assume that you are having a hard time telling us you want to live elsewhere. We have arranged for the movers to take your belongings to Acme Storage Rental, Unit #31, on the first day of the month.

We have rented this storage space for you in your own name and have paid for two months rent as our way of helping you with the transition.

Please know this is in no way a rejection of you on our part, but an expression of our deep love, confidence, and concern for you, as well as our sincere desire to see you happy and independent.

Please accept our best wishes and love,

Mom and Dad

Yes, the youngster who received this letter was angry. He said, "Fine, if that's the way you want it, I'm out of here!"

His parents did not hear one word from or about him for six weeks. Then they heard through his friends that he had moved in with some of his buddies, but they kicked him out because he didn't pay his share of the expenses. He then moved in with some other young men, but they also threw him out.

During the eighth week he called. "Well, I guess you want my phone number."

His mom replied, "Sure, if you want us to have it."

"And I suppose you want to know my address!"

"Sure, if you want us to have it. Thanks for calling. We love you and hope you are doing well."

The following week he called to say, "I suppose you want to know where I'm working."

Needless to say, this young man and his parents now have a much better relationship. Isn't this why we raise children—to produce independent adults who can lead their own happy, independent lives?

Parenting power doesn't mean physical force or abuse.
Jim presents the keys to parenting power in the next article.

↵

Putting Some Power Into Parenting
Volume 9, no. 4

"It works! It works," I heard. Suddenly everyone in the cafeteria was staring at us and wondering what was going on. A gentleman was yelling at me from across the room in Heidelberg, Germany, where my wife and I were eating with two friends. We were all wearing Love and Logic sweatshirts.

Across the room came a man with outstretched hand. "I saw the shirts with the big red heart and knew right away that Love and Logic was back in town. I've been waiting for you to come back to Germany so I could thank you for all you did for my family. Love and Logic has changed our lives!"

"There's no way you would know me," he continued. "I was just one of hundreds of people who attended your Love and Logic workshop the last time you spoke at the military post. But I have to tell you that my kids didn't know what hit them when I got home. Their lives will never be the same."

He went on to tell one of the many stories we heard during that tour. However, the story that told us that our work to break the cycle of child abuse was paying off came from one of the advocates.

Love and Logic training was being offered to many of the parents. Great parents as well as those needing help all came together to learn new skills. Some parents were there to find new ways to break the cycle of child abuse. That's what this story is all about.

As a way of evaluating the success of the Love and Logic training, some social workers interviewed children and parents. One child was asked, "Are things any better for you now that your parents have had Love and Logic training?"

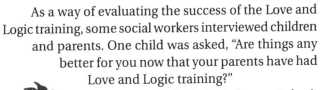

"Oh, I don't know. I don't think so!" he responded.

"That's too bad. Do you mean to tell me that it's not better?" asked the social worker.

"My folks just keep pulling that Jim Fay stuff all the time."

"Well, does your dad still get mad and hit you?"

"No. He never yells at us anymore. And he never hits us anymore. But last night he said the car was leaving at 6:45 and I wasn't ready to go, and they all went to the show without me and I had to walk down to the theater to catch up with them!"

For years we have told parents not to hit their kids. However, this is no help unless we can tell them what to do instead. Love and Logic taught this dad how to get results in a more effective way. So here we have a dad who discovered some new skills that are much more powerful than yelling and hitting. He discovered the power of the enforceable statement and broke his old cycle of child abuse.

The "enforceable statement" tells the child how you are going to run your life instead of telling him how to run his life.

How many times have you heard parents tell their kids to save their allowance? "Don't be in here begging for money. I gave you your allowance yesterday, and you've already wasted it. I get sick and tired of always having to give you additional money because you can't save. Look. I'll give it to you this time, but this is the last time!"

This is a prime example of a parent trying to tell the child how to run his life. You and I know it will do no good. The child learned nothing because he did not have to solve his own problem. The parent will be shelling out more money in just a few days.

A parent using the "enforceable statement" handles the same problem this way: "I'm sorry you're out of money. I'll be giving you more allowance on Saturday as usual."

Any self-respecting child will probably launch into "brain drain" saying, "That's not fair." However, Love and Logic parents know how to handle this type of manipulation. They just play "broken record."

When the child says, "Not fair!" the parent says, "I know," in a very empathetic tone. The parent continues to say, "I know," to each additional complaint and reminds the youngster that he will receive more money on Saturday.

I hope you find that these examples of enforceable and unenforceable statements give you some additional skills as well as the courage to set firm limits for your kids without waging war.

10

Volume 10

I'm 16 Years Old, Where's My Car?
Volume 10, no. 1

Letters such as the following from a Colorado teenager make me leap out of bed each morning eager to teach more parents the art of Love and Logic parenting:

> Dear Mr. Fay:
>
> My parents have read your books and attended one of your classes. I must say this has ruined my life! Every time I ask for something my parents feel is unreasonable, they say, "No!" When I ask why, they say, "Because we love you." I don't know if that's one of your lines, but if it is, thanks a whole lot!
>
> The "no problem" line is even worse. Everything my parents say ends with "no problem." You might call this discipline, but I call it torture! You have ruined all my chances of getting a car. My parents have read your articles in the paper and have taken your advice. Now I don't have a car or even a life! I thank you sincerely. I'm a 4.0 student, responsible, and a great kid. Why shouldn't I have a car?
>
> Please write back explaining why parents should not give their teenagers a car. I'd really appreciate it.
>
> Thanks for your time,
> (Name withheld)

This youngster was reacting to his parents' new parenting style after they read my suggestions on how to make teens totally responsible for their own safe driving.

These parents understand that teen driving is a grave responsibility. For once a teen has a car, he/she is in charge of a deadly weapon capable of killing others, including him/herself. Irresponsible teen driving can have serious consequences for both the teenager, parents and others.

Place responsibility where it belongs

I offer the following guidelines to help parents place the responsibility for safe driving right where it belongs—squarely on the shoulders of the teen. This begins with financial responsibility.

1. Never buy your teenager a car. Teens who have made a financial investment in their cars tend to think, "If I wreck this car, then what am I going to drive?" They relate to financial concerns better than personal injury.

2. Insist that your teen pay the increased costs associated with his/her driving. These range from insurance premiums to gasoline to wear and tear on the car if he/she is driving the family car.

> In the real world, no one ever gives an adult a car for free or pays for the associated costs. Prepare your teen for this reality before adulthood slaps him/her in the face.

3. Be sure your teen, not you, calls insurance agents about insurance coverage, premiums, and discounts for good grades and driver education. Teens tend to take bad news from the insurance agent better than from their parents.

4. Since driving is a new experience for your teen, insist that he/she deposits cash, equal to the insurance deductible on the family car, into your savings account to cover potential repairs. If an accident occurs, this deposit pays for repairs, and your son or daughter does not drive until another deposit is made.

5. What about traffic tickets? Provide lots of sympathy . . . but never pay for the ticket! Parents who pay for tickets are buying lots of big-time trouble. Instead, say, "Let's make a deal, Son. I'll never ask you to pay for my tickets and vice-versa."

6. Be very firm about alcohol or drugs and driving. Tell your teen, "You may use the car as long as I don't ever have to worry about drugs or alcohol."

If you smell even one whiff of alcohol, it's time to announce, "I'm now worrying about the use of alcohol—what's your guess about the car?" When your teen asks when he/she can drive again, say, "I don't know. It's your job to convince me that I no longer have to worry. I'm sure you understand that's not an overnight deal."

How do you reply when your teen asks, "Oh, fine, just fine! How am I supposed to get to work?" You answer, "I don't know. I was going to ask you the same question."

Caution! You lose your campaign to teach responsibility if you rescue the teen at this point. We are no longer talking about minor responsibility. We are now in the big leagues of life-and-death responsibility.

Sixteen can be a great age

You've probably been wondering about my response to the author of the letter who asked me to defend my position on parents not buying cars for their kids. Here is my reply:

Dear Friend,

You sound like a great kid to me. Your letter also indicates that you are responsible and can think for yourself. I'd love to visit with you if you'd like to call me here at the Love and Logic Institute.

To answer your question: I do want teens like you to have cars and to be able to drive. I have learned that kids who earn what they have are much more successful later in life. Teens who invest in their own cars are also much safer drivers and have a longer life expectancy!

The bottom line is that I want you—and others like you—to live a long, happy life and to be around for a long time. America needs teenagers like you to grow up and run the country, not silver-platter kids who haven't learned how succeed through struggle.

As a 16-year-old, this might be difficult for you to understand. When you are older and have a teen of your own, I want you to write me again and let me know things looks then. In the meantime, feel free to call me.

Sincerely,
Jim Fay, President
Cline/Fay Institute, Inc.

Sixteen is a wonderful age. Driving is what makes it so. It's a great relief for parents to have responsible kids who can drive themselves around. It need not be a time to be feared as long as teens are well-trained and prepared for the responsibilities. I hope these suggestions lead to both happy parenting and happy motoring.

If your children drive you crazy while you're on the phone,
you're not alone. In the next article, Jim tells
how one mother taught her children to let her talk in peace!

∽

Don't Inconvenience Mom When She's on the Phone
Volume 10, no. 2

"They're driving me crazy! Every time I'm on the phone they start bickering with each other. If it's not that, they're jerking the cord and asking for something. I haven't had a pleasant phone conversation in months. What's a mother to do?"

Do you get the impression that the children of this frustrated mother are mistaken about who is the most important person in the house? Is it possible they want all mom's attention all the time? Is it possible they don't think it's fair for mom to talk on the phone?

The happiest and most responsible children know, without a doubt, that the parent is the most important person in the house. And they know the parent will not tolerate being interrupted.

These children have learned that hassling the most important person in the house is never in their best interest; when that person is inconvenienced, it means he/she cannot do his/her regular work. And when that person can't do his/her regular work, someone is going to have to pick up the slack. The person who picks up the slack by doing the chores is the one who created the inconvenience in the first place!

Now that you understand the Love and Logic philosophy on inconvenience, you can learn some ways to end your children's constant hassling while you're on the phone. Sometimes this attention-getting behavior requires some very direct and serious training that involves unpleasant consequences.

This is not to say that the most important person in the house is going to be mean to the children. What it does mean is that the most important person in the house is going to take care of him/herself. This could also mean that consequences will be meted out for inconveniencing the most important person in the house.

Use training sessions to change the pattern

The good news is that Love and Logic has some answers for frustrated moms. We don't have to put up with these kinds of interruptions. It is simply not good for children to get by with this kind of misbehavior. Sad but true, when kids get by with inappropriate behavior, it decreases their self-confidence in their ability to control themselves.

Anna is a mom who learned to take care of herself by adopting Love and Logic principles. She doesn't scream at the kids to get her way. She simply announces from time to time how she is going to run her own life. Her kids are forced to find ways to fit into the situation.

Anna's children had discovered that when mom talked on the phone, she didn't give them any direct attention. They didn't like that. So, they would begin fighting every time the phone rang. Or, they would hang on Anna, complaining, bickering, or begging.

Anna decided to do something about this by using a Love and Logic training session. She called one of her friends and explained the problem. Of course, she did this when the kids were not around to hear her plan.

"Paula," said Anna, "my kids are in need of some special training. They are driving me nuts whenever I talk on the phone. Would you be willing to call me, just to visit, several times during the next few days?"

"If the kids are true to form, they'll start right into their routine. Then I'll put you on hold for a few minutes. I'll act like it's no big deal that we're stopping the conversation while I straighten out the kids. That way, they're going to find out that inconveniencing me is a very bad a decision on their part."

"This sounds great!" answered Paula. "Then you can do the same thing for me and all our kids will be trained. But what are you going to say to the kids when you put me on hold?"

Anna started telling Paula about the Love and Logic concept on "inconvenience." "Around this house," she explained, "when the parents are inconvenienced by the kids, we have to spend unnecessary time hassling with them and coming up with solutions to the problems they've caused."

"So, when we're inconvenienced, the time and energy we lose has to be paid back by the kids. They usually do this by scrubbing toilets, washing windows, pulling weeds, or doing some of our other chores."

"Tonight, I'm going to have a little heart-to-heart talk with the kids. I'm going to let them know what a terrible inconvenience it is when they misbehave while I'm on the phone. But I'm not going to warn them about what will happen because I've learned from Jim and Foster that it's best to let them wonder about what I'm going to do.

"I'll just thank them for visiting with me and drop it. Then I'll secretly hope they blow it the next time I'm on the phone. So please call me tomorrow morning. They'll be here and we can have a training session."

Paula called the next morning. True to form, the kids started in on Anna. Very politely Anna said, "Oh, Paula, I'm so sorry. Would you please hold? We're about to have a Love and Logic moment here at our house."

Anna put the phone down, calmly walked over to her children and said in a stern voice: "I told you that bothering me while I'm on the phone is a real inconvenience. Now I'm going to do something about this! Where do you want to wait until I have time to finish my visit with Paula and figure out how you're going to pay me back? Do you want to wait in your room or in the family room? If you can't decide, I'll be happy to choose for you."

The kids stayed in the family room while Anna finished her visit with Paula. They paid their mom back for the inconvenience by pulling weeds that same afternoon. This left Anna and Paula more time to giggle on the phone over how well Love and Logic works in situations like this.

Now when the children forget and annoy mom while she's on the phone, she turns to them and asks, "Are you sure you want to inconvenience me?" This is usually followed by a quick retreat by the kids.

The beauty of the "inconvenience" technique is that it can be adapted to all kinds of situations. I invite you to experiment with this technique and then write to me about your results. Maybe your creative use of "inconvenience" will appear in a future Love and Logic Journal. Have fun with your Love and Logic kids.

Are you afraid to hold your children accountable for their behavior?
In the next article, Jim shows how you can regain credibility with your children.

∽

Parents Who Cry Wolf
Volume 10, no. 3

The owner of the campground had spent considerable time, energy, and expense to spread colored gravel in the picnic area. It was clean and beautiful. But it would not be clean and beautiful for long.

Eight-year-old Dennis was systematically destroying the owner's hard work. He was scooping up the gravel and launching it into the bushes beyond the retaining logs.

How did I know his name was Dennis? I heard his parents yelling at him over and over as they pleaded, begged, and threatened.

"Dennis, eat your hot dog, you're going to be hungry. Dennis, how many times do I have to tell you? Dennis your food is getting cold! Dennis, are we going to have to get mad? Dennis, am I going to have to spank you? Dennis, are we going to have to leave you home next time? Dennis, why can't you just cooperate for once!"

Notice that not once did these parents express any concern for the damage Dennis was doing. And, they did not follow through with any of their hollow threats. They reminded me of the boy in the story, "The Boy Who Cried Wolf." Their words no longer had any credibility in their son's eyes.

I seriously doubt they had ever followed through with any of their previous demands or threats. Here is a child who knows his parents are either afraid to hold him accountable for his actions or just don't know how.

Dennis' mom finally said, "Stop throwing that gravel!" At this point Dennis sported a sly little grin that is typical of spoiled kids who know they are getting away with their antics. He was having a great time frustrating his parents.

Dennis stopped for about 60 seconds and then began scooping up the gravel again. But this time, he did it with his feet. Mom yelled, "I told you to stop throwing that gravel!"

"I'm not throwing anything. My hands are in my pockets. Jeez!"

At this point, Mom just rolled her eyes and ignored his behavior. She looked at my wife and me with that resigned kind of look that says, "What are you going to do with kids these days?"

I would liked to have said, "You can do plenty! No parent should put up with that kind of behavior. Allowing kids to misbehave is very damaging to them. It convinces them that they are incapable of controlling themselves."

Children whose parents provide no limits or controls become very insecure. They constantly act out. It is almost as if they are saying with their actions, "How bad do I have to act before you'll set some limits for me? Please love me enough to set some limits!"

Never too late

It is never too late to change this pattern. Parents who apply Love and Logic techniques report that their child's age makes very little difference. That's because we don't change the child with Love and Logic, we change the parent. That's something the parent has control over.

Even though Dennis' parents had been permissive in the past, they could still have taken charge of him that evening in the picnic area. It would have been a shock to Dennis, and he probably would have pitched a fit to get them to back off. However, the fact that a child cries or has a fit doesn't mean the parents are wrong or need to give in.

First of all, I would have advised the parents to take Dennis gently by the hand and go for a short walk. Then they should have gotten right in his face and said softly, "Dennis, I expect you to get your act together, quit throwing the gravel, and eat like you're supposed to. Thank you. You may return to the table now."

My educated guess is that Dennis would have tried everything he could think of to avoid cooperating. If so, the parents should have led him back to the camper and told him that dinner was over. He could try eating politely again at breakfast.

There is no doubt Dennis would try to manipulate his parents into feeding him later when he got hungry. But this is a time the parents cannot give in. This is a time for Dennis to live with his bad decisions. No amount of pleading, begging, or manipulation should work for him.

Yes, this means an uncomfortable evening for the parents. However, no rewards come to parents who are not willing to pay the price.

The parents could also have contacted the campground manager and asked for some support: "I will be bringing Dennis down to the office before breakfast to ask how he can pay for the damage he did to the picnic area. Please don't tell him to forget it. Charge him the going rate for the repairs. I'll pay and then get the money from him at home. This may be a good time for Dennis to convert some toys into cash."

Even though Dennis has been out of control for eight years, he will have learned today that things are going to change in this family. It may take several learning opportunities before it totally sinks in. However, in the future, each time his parents ask for something, Dennis may think, "Uh oh, I bet they are going to do something if I don't watch out."

As you read this, you may be thinking of other parents you know who are in the same situation. They are often afraid to say "no" to their children, or they are afraid to do something when their kids misbehave.

This situation develops in families in which parents give orders that they either can't or won't enforce. Little by little, their children learn that orders mean nothing. Their parents' word becomes garbage.

What to do?

1. Never tell a child to do something unless you intend to follow through.

2. If a child refuses, do something about it. Take him/her by the hand and go a different room or location to help break the emotional spell of the moment.

> Then get right in your child's face. Lower the volume of your voice and say with determination, "That's enough of that. I expect you to . . ."

> Then, with even more determination and an even lower voice, say, "Now! Do you think it would be wise for you to continue acting that way? Get back in there and show me that you can behave. Thank you!"

3. If you can't think of a good consequence for a youngster's misbehavior, try this: "This is a real inconvenience. I'm going to have to do something about this. I'll let you know what it is going to be."

> Later, when your head is clear, announce to your child how he/she can pay you back for the inconvenience. Remember, when parents are inconvenienced, it means they've had to spend a lot of extra time figuring out what to do about the inconvenience. This means they are not able to get their regular work done.

The best way the child can pay the parents back is by taking care of some of the parents' chores. The parent guarantees the chore will be done by saying to the youngster, "Take your time folding the laundry. Just have it done before your next meal. That could be today, tomorrow, or Saturday. You decide."

Of course, none of these techniques will work if the parent is the kind of person who cries wolf. You must be prepared to follow through and make sure your words are as good as gold.

The happiest and most responsible children I know have parents who mean what they say. These children don't waste time testing their parents to see if they are really serious.

In the following article, Jim explains why
pampered children seldom grow up to lead happy lives.

∽

The Permissiveness Trap
Volume 10, no. 4

Your friend, Marge, has just picked you up for a luncheon engagement. As you walk toward her car, she says, "I hope you don't mind. I brought my 9-year-old son along. He hates to stay with baby sitters."

You're not sure what to say, but you can hardly say no at this point because he is already here. It's a "done deal" and you had no choice.

As you near the car, you hear the car stereo blasting out from the car even through the closed windows. You and your friend enter the car and she drives off. The music is still blasting.

Marge says nothing to her child about the volume of the music. The two of you try to visit, but you have to yell to be heard. Finally you say, "Do you suppose we could turn down the radio? I'm having a hard time hearing you."

Marge answers, "Jason likes the music that way."

At this point you are losing your appreciation for Jason and say, "But what about you? Do you like it that loud?"

Marge replies, "Jason is the most important thing in my life. I can put up with a few annoyances so he will know how much I love him. Besides, I have been studying Love and Logic parenting and it says you have to give your kids choices. And besides that, he gets so mad when I don't let him decide about things. I don't want him to grow up to hate me."

What's wrong with Marge's thinking?

Marge has fallen into the trap called "the child-centered environment." Children who are treated as though they are the most important people in the family become increasingly self-centered and selfish. These children become more and more demanding and hostile when they don't get their way and are only happy when being pampered.

These pampered children develop a false sense of importance while at the same time becoming very insecure about achieving on their own or solving their own problems through struggle. As they grow older they are more and more inclined to blame their problems on others.

These children become little tyrants who are not fun to live with, especially when they become teens. They don't return their parents' love, while at the same time they complain their parents don't demonstrate enough love for them.

Notice that Marge is already afraid to cross Jason. She is willing to set aside her own needs in favor of his. She says this is because she wants Jason to know how much she loves him. My guess is that she has been manipulated into this position by Jason, who withholds his love when he wishes to punish Marge and get his way.

How often do you think Jason manipulates Marge into giving in to him with statements such as, "I hate you!" or, "If you loved me you would . . . "

Pampered children seldom grow up to lead happy lives

The child-centered environment creates more problems. One of these has to do with the issue of modeling. Children learn how to be adults by subconsciously imitating the most important adults in their lives. This helps to explain why we grow up to have many of the values, mannerisms, and habits of our parents even when we did not especially like our parents' traits.

It should be no surprise that pampered children do not grow up to be happy. They usually don't grow up to take good care of themselves. After years of watching their parents sacrifice their own needs and happiness in favor of the children, they learn to do the same thing.

There is an additional problem as these children grow up to be parents. They add a little twist that increases their own sense of unhappiness. Since they grew up to believe that others are responsible for their happiness, they do a lot of complaining to their children. Rather than taking good care of themselves, they spend a lot of time saying, "You're driving me crazy," "Why can't you just behave once in awhile?" or, "I can't understand it. I've given you everything, and this is the way you pay me back!"

Kids need to see their parents taking care of themselves. They need to see the parents creating their own happiness. They need to see their parents treating themselves as important. If they don't see this, they will not know how to do it for themselves. You can't model these traits and treat the child as the most important person in the house at the same time.

Parents who pamper their children steal away their child's ability to achieve through struggle

Today's children will grow into a world in which there will be many unpredictable challenges. To be prepared to face this world, they will need to believe they can solve new and different problems through determination and hard work.

People who believe they can survive adversity through struggle are those who have done it over and over again. Their parents did not serve happiness and success on a silver platter. Their parents were strong people who gave good advice and backed off, allowing their children to practice for the real world by solving their own problems through struggle and determination.

Be sure your children have the advantage of knowing that as Americans, they have the right to life, liberty, and the pursuit of happiness. They don't have the right to happiness served on a silver platter.

Marge is confused about the use of choices

Marge explained away her permissiveness with Jason by saying she has studied Love and Logic. She claimed that Love and Logic advocates choices. Marge also noted that Jason gets mad when he doesn't get to decide things.

Never allow children to make decisions that affect others

Love and Logic parents never allow a child to make decisions that affect anyone other than himself. In others words, children don't make decisions about adult issues such as how money is spent, how the parents spend their time, etc. Therefore, a youngster doesn't get to decide that everyone in the house listens to his loud music. The appropriate child's decision should be whether the music is played softly or whether it is played over earphones.

Never allow children to make a decision unless you are willing to allow them to live with the consequences of that decision

The only kids who demand to make adult decisions are those who have been making the wrong kinds of decisions. They have started out their lives making adult decisions and become addicted to being in total control. Then they become like Jason, who gets mad when he can't decide everything.

Marge should have started Jason out with tiny decisions such as the color of his socks. Instead she started him with big decisions that determine the quality of her life. Now Jason is spoiled.

Kids don't need to make big decisions. They are happy with small ones. Give them many small decisions to make. Do it as often as you can. Then when you need to make the big decisions, you can say, "Wait a minute, Jason. Don't I usually let you decide? I do, don't I? Now it's my turn to decide. Thanks for understanding."

Permissive parents allow their children to make all the decisions they want to make. They also don't require their children to live with the consequences of the decisions they make.

Love and Logic parents allow children to make the decisions that affect them only. And they require their children to live with consequences of the decisions they make. Marge fell into the trap of the child-centered environment. Don't let it happen to you.

SECTION TWO

Foster W. Cline, M.D.

11

Volume 1

Foster W. Cline, M.D. did not contribute an article to Volume 1, no. 1

✍

School Problems and Children
Volume 1, no. 2

With the opening of school each fall, the familiar parental litany of lamentations begins: "John has poor study habits . . . " "George doesn't seem to care about his grades, and nothing I do seems to help." "Susan can't understand that her future is based on what she does now . . . ," or "Jeff is very bright but just does average work or less! He doesn't come close to his potential."

What can parents do to avoid these trials? Are they normal? Do they have to happen? The answer is, "Yes, they are normal and they are absolutely unnecessary!" Families need not experience the painful times centered around school work.

Modeling is important

The way adults live rubs off on their children. I often hear parents complain about their children's study habits. Then I find out the house has two or three color TV sets but no set of encyclopedias! No wonder their children don't care about books.

On the other hand, one dad, a physician, does some of his charting and dictation at home. He notes to his third-grader, "It feels so good to be done with my homework!" Now that's setting an example!

The more parents worry, the less kids worry

There is a reciprocal relationship around "units of concern." There are only ten units per family. If Mom or Dad worries six or seven units worth about school and homework, you can bet the children only worry three or four units worth!

Because life is generally a great reciprocal relationship, we can say that worried parents raise worrisome kids. The more time mom is at school taking care of things, the more her child needs to be taken care of. It's not too long until mom truthfully says, "I have to be at school because Roger is so immature!"

Of course, why would any of us grow up if we had a mom literally taking care of everything. Non-worried parents are best at raising kids who take care of their own future. Such parents can easily say, "Well, John, no big sweat. They hold fourth grade every year. No matter how many times you have to take fourth, I'll love you lots!"

Rules about rules

Ideally, parents should not set rules about school work. Some day, when the child goes to college, he/she is going to have to live without any parental rules—and the sooner the better. Of course, when children are very small, we need to set rules.

Nevertheless, we strive for the ideal of no rules. Parents who set many rules tend to wear themselves out checking to see whether or not they are being followed. The fewer the rules, the less checking and the easier the parenting job!

Rules shouldn't be confused with love and concern. If I express concern over the way homework is being done, I have nothing to check. As soon as I make rules about the way homework is to be done, then I'm very busy. Many children from homes with lots of rules go off to college and flunk their first semester—because suddenly they have no rules!

Remember these four rules for rules:

1. The fewer the rules the better.
2. Those rules that are made must be enforceable.
3. Those rules that are made are enforced.
4. Consequences for breaking a rule should "fit the crime."
   Sometimes parents must be very creative here.

Now let's take a look at some "reasonable" rules: Joyce, age 8, had trouble doing both her school work and homework. Her parents used the "rant and rave" technique for about a year until they realized it only made things worse.

When Joyce entered third grade, her parents decided to turn things around. They gave the teacher a little pad with sheets pre-printed with the slogan, "No heavy thinking needed, OK for TV."

If Joyce had a good day at school, doing either her school work and/or her previous night's homework, the teacher gave her a slip. That evening she could watch as much TV as she wished. No heaving thinking was needed. If Joyce did not receive the slip on Friday, she watched no TV until the following Monday.

Joyce's father beamed, "This worked like magic. And it kept Harriet and me out of the teacher's hair and wondering what was going wrong. We didn't have to ask any questions. If there was a problem, and it was something that needed heavy thinking, then Joyce could figure it out herself."

The same technique can be used for skiing or other activities the child enjoys. It's important that the parents communicate in a way so the child knows they are taking care of themselves first: "George, when I pay for you to go skiing, it's because I'm doing an average or good job at work. And when I know that you're kissing off school, then I feel like a patsy. I don't feel good about spending money on you because I'm doing my job but you're not doing an average job at yours!"

Common sense and caution must be used, however, before parents take away activities that raise a child's self-image. Study after study shows that a high self-image is much more reliable than grades in predicting future success. If a child has a poor self-image around school work and boosts his image through sports, parents do not help the situation by taking away sports.

Foster explores the overlooked issue of parental self-esteem in the next article.

The Importance of Parental Basic Trust and Self-esteem
Volume 1, no. 3

Much has been written about the importance of self-esteem in children. Not enough has been written about the importance of self-esteem and basic trust in parents. Frankly, there are three great feelings that almost always have a high correlation: high self-esteem, high sense of basic trust, and low feelings of guilt.

When our own self-esteem is low, we are more likely to try to live our lives vicariously through other people, such as movie stars or our children!

Our children's successes then become our own successes. Unfortunately, our children pick up on this and begin to feel they are not living for themselves. They usually choose one of two responses: they either quit achieving, or they continue to achieve but distance themselves from their parents.

Parents can live through their children's successes in elementary school, but it simply won't work in late junior high and high school. Wise parents are proud for their children's successes and admire their accomplishments. They tend, with humility, to give God, faith, and luck a great deal of the credit. Most of all, their child gets the credit.

When parents have a high sense of basic trust, it allows them to set fewer rules. Such parents know that things tend to work out well without their tight control. At the same time, parents who have a low sense of guilt can easily enforce the rules that are set.

Those parents who lack basic trust and who tend to feel guilty have a tough time with their children. They do a great deal of threatening and rule-setting but have a hard time following through. Such a parent might say, "You're grounded for a month," but then relent after two weeks. Teenagers lose respect for these adults. This reinforces the parent's low self-esteem, and the whole situation turns into a vicious circle.

If parental self-esteem is coupled with a high sense of basic trust, the following statements are self-evident and easy to follow. If self-esteem is lacking or there is a poor sense of basic trust, then these statements may not make as much sense or may be more difficult to carry out:

1. I know my child will grow as I am. I can never teach self-esteem, I can only model it.

2. I trust that things generally tend to work out well and therefore intervene with rules only when absolutely necessary.

3. I know my child, like a flower, will open from the inside when showered with love and opportunity. I must never try to force the petals open by prying into the child's life and trying to force a flowering of success.

4. I know my child's personality and value system, for better or for worse, is largely formed by age 11. After age 11, I need to trust my upbringing and genetics.

5. Telling a child how I feel and think about a situation is generally more effective than telling the child how to think and behave.

6. I know that by giving my child the right to fail, he or she will probably choose success. If I try to force success, the child is more likely to choose failure. It's a paradox.

7. My joyous participation in my child's life and achievements will do more than any other one thing towards building his or her pride in those accomplishments.

8. Generally, three-fourths of my relationship with my child will be spent as one adult with another. How this relationship turns out must be primary in my mind. Always, I will work toward developing a lasting friendship.

9. Most of us have learned our lessons through consequences. Therefore, I can only hope that my child makes lots of mistakes while young and while consequences are seldom life-threatening.

10. I will always show my child more pizazz and excitement over things done well than anger and disappointment over things done poorly. My child will always go for the emotion.

The above 10 points are not parental commandments. They are simply realizations, that, when acted upon, cannot help but enhance self-esteem.

Are report cards important? Foster discusses
how to handle them beginning on the next page.

Are report cards important? Foster discusses
how to handle them beginning on the next page.

Rules For Handling Report Cards
Volume 1, no. 4

Our youngsters are back in school. It won't be long until we get their report cards. Right? Wrong! We don't get the reports cards. They do! That's the point. In fact, it brings us to the first rule about report cards: Keep the monkey on the child's back.

It's important that children know that report cards are their business. As parents, we care. Our caring might even shade into concern. But worry? That's the child's job.

I'll never forget how my wise old dad always kept the report card problem on my back. As a young child, I had a pretty severe learning disorder. As a student at Park Hill Elementary School in Denver, I came home with straight "D's."

My dad would always look over the report card, and taking our his fat, black fountain pen, would ask, "Son, are you proud of this?" I would inevitably answer, "No, sir." And then he'd say, "That's good, Son," and sign the card.

Heaven help me if I had ever said I was proud of the report card. I would have had tutoring, private schooling, and heaven knows what all.

The feelings and performance equation

The following algebraic equation of feelings and performance always holds true:

When a child feels good (plus) about his/her good work (plus), the result is positive $(+ \times + = +)$.

When a child gets good grades (plus) but even then feels bad about him/herself (minus), the long-term outcome may be poor in spite of the grades $(+ \times - = -)$.

When a child does poorly (minus) and feels bad about doing poorly (minus) we simply don't have to worry because things will eventually work out well $(- \times - = +)$.

When a child does poorly (minus), but feels fine about doing poorly (plus), the result is a negative minus $(+ \times - = -)$.

We can sum up the algebraic equation routine simply by noting that when a child performs like a turkey, he or she often wishes to become an eagle. But when a child performs like a turkey and feels like an eagle, he doesn't fly very far!

Show more excitement about high grades than low grades

Children want pizazz. They love and crave parental emotions. On an unconscious level, it doesn't matter whether the parent's emotion is about great things or poor things.

A parent who handles things well might say, "Hey, hey, hey! A big 'A' in art! Wow, a 'B' in gym. Well, of course you always did run like the wind. Hey a big 'B' in typing. You'll probably be able to turn out papers quickly. That's important. Humm, a 'D' in math. Well, I suppose that could be better. Wow, a big 'B' in social studies. It's important to know history! Then non-emotionally the parent asks, "How are you going to handle the math?"

Get involved in the areas in which your child excels

If your child does well in biology, spend some time at the pond and look at critters through a microscope. If your child does well in math, find out if the harmonics of the solar system interest him. If your child does well in history, read a book on World War II.

Too many adults concentrate on a youngster's weaknesses. But as adults, we tend to avoid people who concentrate on our weaknesses. That's called divorce!

Explore poor grades in a non-emotional but caring way

"Humm, do you have any plan for history, kiddo? What are your thoughts on the history grade? Do you think it will improve with time, or continue to go downhill?" It's important that this questioning is not done in a "witness stand" manner.

Poor grades are not the problem; the reason for the poor grades is the problem

Children get poor grades because of a poor self-image (translation: "He's lazy"); because of rebellion against their parents' value system (translation: "He's lazy"); because of anxiety (translation: "He's a sensitive child); or because of depression, learning problems, and a host of other reasons. Sometimes it's wise to have an outsider look at the child and help the parents decide on an appropriate response.

Sometimes a child has an attitude problem. And sometimes we need to accept that. One evening my eldest daughter said, "I hate algebra. I'm not going to look at the problems. I'm not even going to try to do my homework!"

Such a poor attitude, out of character for Robin, surprised me. In my parental wisdom, I replied, "Well, Robin, your attitude kind of surprises me. Would you like some help on your algebra tonight?" She brightened up immediately, answering, "Oh sure, Dad. Gee, thanks!"

So I read the problem. It asked for the amount of kinetic energy with which a rocket hits the earth, considering it reached a certain perigee and had a certain momentum of so many kilograms per kilometer. Finally I worked out an answer. I was pretty proud of myself until Robin checked my answer with those listed in the back of the book. I had forgotten that some books actually provide the answers in the back! My answer was dead wrong!

I worked the problem again. The answer was wrong again. Half an hour later I said, "I hate algebra! I never liked it. I've always had problems with it. Shut the darn book! Ask your teacher how to do it tomorrow!" At that point I realized how reasonable her earlier bad attitude had been. I simply did not understand it at the time!

Help your child learn good study habits in a non-demanding way

Every child needs his/her own place to study and a non-angry expectation that he/she will spend time at that spot, thinking about homework. This is important whether or not he/she does the homework.

It's easy to get into big control battles over homework. But we can avoid them when we give a child an opportunity at least to think about his/her homework and perhaps decide to do it during that time.

Supervise improvement in school work only when absolutely necessary

I hate supervising other people. I hate it when others supervise me! Adults don't like being monitored by anyone.

But sometimes it's necessary. I know that if I'm forced to monitor my child now, he/she many grow up believing that monitoring is necessary as an adult. Some poor spouse may be forced to do the supervising down the road. I'd like to get totally out of the monitoring business.

In rare cases, it may be necessary to encourage improvement. If it is, I'll do it. But, if I'm still monitoring my child's achievement by high school, the game is pretty well lost. I'll have to hand the monitoring function over to his/her first spouse to carry out during the first unsuccessful marriage.

Finally, we can always help our child with school work as long as it's fun for us! Never continue past that point. It sends a message of frustration. But our children don't understand that it is our frustration. They read it as our frustration over them personally.

12
Volume 2

How Loving Parents Can Raise Children With Low Self-images
Volume 2, no. 1

We all know that self-image plays the primary role in high achievement. In fact, study after study shows that self-image is a far more important factor in achievement than either intelligence or gifts from the environment ("lucky breaks").

We also know that the ability to love and the joy of being loved play primary roles in self-image. Therefore, it appears paradoxical that many children with poor self-images are raised in loving families. It does not take a clinical genius to understand that angry, unloving, and negative parents tend to raise children with poor self-images. But how do the good, loving parents bring that about?

In my years of clinical practice, I have noticed three ways many parents unknowingly cause problems for their children.

1. Over-reassurance and over-attention to nerd behavior

In the name of helping children understand themselves and a particular situation, I have seen many adults give a child a long explanation. A simple and immediate consequence would have been far more effective and less traumatic for the child.

For instance, as two siblings somewhat obnoxiously played with their food at a fast food restaurant, their parents responded by giving them a long dissertation: "That behavior isn't nice. Mommy doesn't like that when we're in public. " (I guess it would be OK to act like that at home!)

At any rate, instead of a dissertation on proper behavior, it would have been far more effective simply to send the children out to the car and let them wait there until the parents were finished eating. It also would have been effective to give the kids a couple of choices: "Would you rather stay here and eat nicely, or would you rather wait for us in the car?"

Parents also tend to give dissertations in response to the following statement by a child: "You don't like me!" The parent responds by reassuring the child of his/her love, explaining why he/she doesn't like that type of talk, or presenting why it's not nice.

In reality, it would be better to simply say, "I'm sorry you feel that way. I hope you change your mind. Bringing it up more than once a week is tacky. Please go to your room and give it some deeper thought."

Another example of over-reassurance often takes place when a child comes to our office to see one of the therapists. Just as the child is ready to go into the office, I often hear a parent say, "It'll be OK," in a reassuring tone. Once a child hears that, it validates the very likelihood that it might not be OK, or the parent would never have provided the reassurance. Whenever a parents says, "It'll be OK," in a doctor's office, one can almost be sure the child will stay glued to the waiting room seat.

Children often hook their parents into giving dissertations. When a child does a fair or even poor job on a paper, all he/she has to do to receive a long, loving dissertation on the basic goodness of the paper is to say, "I don't think it's any good!" The parents then go into a long speech about the value of the paper.

Nerd behavior is nerd behavior. We need not be reassuring about it. When children say negative things it is usually much better for parents to say, "I hope you change your mind. Glad I don't feel like that about the things I do!"

2. Putting the clamps on teens

So often loving parents do a really good job of raising elementary school children. They treat their youngsters as though they were mature. The parent/child relationship is solid.

Suddenly, when the children reaches adolescence, the parents either unconsciously or consciously become frightened: "Now they're older and can get into more trouble—I'd better clamp down!"

The parents would be wiser to think, "I trust my parenting techniques. The kid's probably OK. He's older now and can probably think better. Good Luck, Roger!"

I remember one little girl who said to me with tears, "When I was 8 years old, I didn't have to tell my mother where I was every minute. And when I was 8 years old, I didn't have to let my mother meet my friends. And when I was 8 years old, I could be late for dinner. It's not my fault I grew boobs, Dr. Cline. Every girl grows boobs!"

The girl was right. She curved out and her parents clamped down. This needless clamping down is often the cause of a great deal of adolescent turmoil and poor self-image as well as family disagreements.

3. Allowing the child to be disrespectful to the parents

As parents, we always get back what we dish out. And children never need to feel any guilt about that! In other words, if I'm often rude and disrespectful to my children, it does not lower their self-images one bit for them to be rude and disrespectful back to me. They know I deserve it!

On the other hand, I occasionally see loving, quiet, overly-giving parents allowing their children to treat them with disrespect. This always causes guilt in youngsters. Even though children avoid letting us see their guilt, that guilt can lead to a poor self-image. A poor self-image, in turn, can lead to internalized anger and problem behavior. The result is a vicious cycle.

When children are disrespectful to their parents, it's best for the parents simply to ask themselves, "Would I allow a neighbor to talk to me this way in my home?" If not, the youngster is getting away with too much. On the other hand, we should always talk to our children as we would talk to good neighbors. It works both ways.

Do not be reassuring when children bad-mouth themselves or their work. Loosen up with as few rules as possible when your good child hits adolescence, and always expect and insist on the same respect you dish out.

Foster shares how to spend some memorable time with your kids in the next article!

◢◠つ

Summer Fun With Your Kids
Volume 2, no. 2

Summer. I hear the TV ads: "Get your kids a computer so they won't be underfoot." The message is loud and clear: Kids are a distraction. Get rid of them. My wife wondered aloud the other day how many kids pick up on that message and actually believe it.

As a child, I always awaited summer with excitement. My parents never considered me underfoot. They were masters at taking care of themselves. I'm sure that if my brother and I were ever underfoot, they would simply tell us to whip off and examine someone else's toes.

But they were enablers. They helped us have fun. They never said "no" unless it was a matter of life and death. Each summer, the lawns on our street would turn dry after the neighborhood kids screwed all the lawn hoses together and stretched them down the block. We'd watch them slither up and down the alley like snakes. We'd talk through them. There were command phones stretching from our back yard at command central, five houses down to a battalion headquarters at Lucky Maxwell's. Another hose snaked four houses over to the FBI home office that Cynthia Howell manned. We raced around the neighborhood, good guys chasing bad, based on the latest intelligence reports from our outposts.

Good memories. Glad my folks cared more about us than always having those hoses neatly tucked away. Thanks folks!

Living near City Park, we naturally spent a lot of time there each summer. We forded the moat around Monkey Island, and when no one was around, we'd sneak into the little Monkey Island house, whip through a tunnel beneath the moat, and then hassle the spider monkeys in their cages. Nothing is as much fun as hassling spider monkeys! They'd have fits, hiss, and spit at us. We'd do it back. At those moments, it was anyone's guess who was the higher primate.

Once we got caught by a big, blue-uniformed police man. He snuck up behind us. If we hadn't been hissing so much, we would have heard him. "Having fun, boys?" We whirled around. "Oh, gee, busted!" He took us to the squad car and told all three of us that he was taking us to the station house for booking.

My little brother began crying up a storm. (He's a judge now in Alaska.) Lucky Maxwell was pretty darn upset, and my own lip was shaking like protoplasmic jelly.

I think the cop took pity on us because of my brother's blubbering. He couldn't handle such massive sorrow, so he said, "Don't worry, when we book you, we'll call your moms, and they can come down and spring you."

My little brother was real polite in such tough situations. Otherwise his tongue was so acid it would burn hardened vanadium. He makes a great lawyer. He gulped through his sobs, "Sir, our mom won't pick us up. She'll say that if you get yourselves into jail, you can get yourselves out! She won't come, office . . . sir!"

The cop immediately swung the car around and took us back to the bird house to pick up our bikes. I know what was cooking through his neurons: "I don't need to deal with that kind of lady today," he was thinking. Mom always separated out who had the problem. It sure saved our necks that day. And it always helped us give some heavy thought to consequences. We never hassled the spider monkeys again. Thanks, Mom!

Have fun with your kids this summer. Get 'em a computer if it helps you relate and enjoy your time together.

Learn to make bedtime hassle-free in Foster's next article.

ᴗᴑ

"Time For Bed, Sweetie"
Volume 2, no. 3

Sometimes bedtime is a hassle. The parent says, "Time for bed, Sweetie." Now what? Kids often have an exciting array of ways to say no: "I don't wanna," "After this program ends;" "Can I have some ice cream first?" and "Read me a story."

This article presents five guidelines that will lead to easier bedtimes.

Guideline 1
DIFFERENT CHILDREN REQUIRE DIFFERENT AMOUNTS OF SLEEP

My mother was a great believer in the idea that children need ten hours of sleep. Period. I don't know where this came from—maybe out of the air!

If fact, my early childhood memories are filled with visions of unneeded nap times. My brother and I would rub our "sleepy" eyes until they looked plenty red. Then we'd stumble out in the afternoon, grope our way into our mom's room, and say, "We just woke up. Can we get up now?" At a very young age, we quickly caught on to the fact that we could get up as long as we had slept. However, if we simply wanted to get up because we didn't need sleep, that was prohibited.

Recent research shows that brighter children, particularly gifted children, may not need as much sleep as others. Too bad. They are bright enough to be more of a problem when they're awake.

Some parents put their kids to bed simply to get them out of their hair in the evening. That's sad. Ideally, the child should be able to be up and not be a bother to his/her parents—at the same time.

On the other hand, if adults need privacy in the evening, sending the children to their rooms is more reasonable than sending them to bed early. It's definitely degrading to have to read with a flashlight under the covers—at any age.

Guideline 2
UNDERSTAND THE REASON YOUR CHILD DOES NOT WANT TO GO TO BED

Sometimes younger children are afraid. Night is associated with scary things. The devil is the lord of blackness. Every kid knows that night creatures are not your basic friendly puppies.

Children have fairly active imaginations. One little 7-year-old girl, after being adopted, imagined that her parents only looked like humans. At night, she believed, their skin would peel off and they would become lizards underneath—shades of *The Visitors*. After all, horror stories touch something present within us all!

Sleep may have other subconscious or unconscious implications. Last year, I saw a 10-year-old who couldn't sleep when his mother had her boyfriend at the house. He imagined his mother running away with the boyfriend. These were fears the mother could have explored with her son.

Some children avoid going to bed if they know their parents will fight as soon as they are out of sight. So, fear of the dark, fear of loss, fear of the unknown, and fear of death may all play roles in a child's bedtime problems.

Guideline 3

EXPLORE A CHILD'S NEGATIVE EMOTIONS IN A FACTUAL, UNDERSTANDING WAY WITHOUT BECOMING EMOTIONALLY INVOLVED

A parent's calm nature usually rubs off on a child. Children's problems usually become more severe if parents become emotionally involved, i.e., exasperated, angry, pleading or frustrated.

An important rule of thumb to remember: As soon as a conversation about a particular issue becomes predictable, or the outcome becomes predictably poor, the issue should be dropped. (This rule could also help many couple relationships.)

The reasons a child does not want to go to bed are not excuses. But just because a youngster is afraid of monsters is no excuse for going to bed late. Your simple, calm reassurance, coupled with the expectation that the child will be able to handle his/her own problem helps. "Luckily, only one kid in 10 million will die in their sleep tonight," or "Most people, when they get old, don't mind dying so much." Or, "It's been over 100 years since a monster was spotted in Denver."

Instead of giving simple reassurances, an over-exploring or overly-involved parent may elevate the ridiculous to the sublime. Pleading, "Ricky, you'll be all right, honey," just makes things worse. It also doesn't improve the situation when parents look under the bed to see if there are any monsters around.

Guideline 4

TAKE ADVANTAGE OF MAGICAL THINKING

Little children really do believe in magic. Some adults do too. Remember the garlic and silver crucifix used for werewolves? It's very reassuring for a little child to have a basic ghostbusting teddy bear on the shelf. Sometimes only one molecule of mom's magic perfume on the upper left corner of the sheet helps a child sleep. Again, such techniques must be used in a light-hearted, caring way that takes advantage of the ways children naturally think.

Remember to avoid being overly-dramatic. If parents do not overly invest in the above ploys, and others, like Puff the Magic Dragon and the Velveteen Rabbit, they will naturally be discarded as the child matures.

Guideline 5

GIVE THE PROPER PHYSICAL SUPPORT

A nightlight or bulb in the hallway or bathroom may be helpful to a child. Small bulbs require only a negligible amount of electricity. It's OK for parents to give in on this issue. But they should stay firm on asking their child to refrain from coming into their bedroom and waking them up because they are afraid. This is a definite no-no! "Look kid, if I get scared, I promise I won't wake you up either!"

If parents don't make bedtime into a big issue, most kids will naturally go to bed when they get sleepy. When our three grown children were small, we would let them fall asleep in the living room and then wake them up and walk them up to their rooms when we went to bed. It didn't take them long to decide that they didn't want to be awakened. They decided on their own to go to bed earlier. No big deal.

Is your child's room a mess? Learn the guidelines
for an appropraite degree of cleanliness in the next article.

✍

The Child's Room

Volume 2, no. 4

The condition of a child's room or the degree of "health hazard" it presents may be the cause of a great deal of parent/child unhappiness. How much effort parents need to expend on the "condition of the sty" really depends on the maturity level of the child and other factors. This article shares three guidelines for handling children's rooms.

Guideline 1

TODDLERS AND PRESCHOOLERS CAN BE TAUGHT THE JOB OF A CLEAN ROOM BY PARENTAL EXAMPLE

Between the ages of two and six, a child internalizes his parents' value systems. That is, the parents' values become the values of the child. Internalization of the value of cleanliness takes place in several ways:

1. The parent shows great joy about cleaning his/her own bedroom. "Boy, do I like having a clean space to lay my head! I just don't sleep well when things are a mess!"

2. The parent has fun cleaning the preschooler's room with the child helping as much as possible. "OK, I'll pick up the blocks and throw them to you. You catch them and put them away . . . Good catch!"

Guideline 2

IDEALLY, BY THE TIME CHILDREN REACH LATE ELEMENTARY SCHOOL, THE CONDITION OF THEIR ROOM IS THEIR OWN CONCERN

By the time children are eight years or older, the problem of a clean room belongs only to them. As a rule of thumb, the parental value system is locked in place by age eleven. If children have been taught the importance of neatness and tidiness and appear to have "forgotten" this in later childhood, parents need not be too concerned. They need only continue taking good care of themselves.

The children should help keep family areas clean, pick up after themselves and do their chores. All of these things directly affect the parents. Parents are not affected directly by the state of their child's room until fleas start hopping out, rats migrate in and out, or it becomes an area health hazard.

This guideline is difficult for many parents. One mother said to me, "Well, I just can't help but open the door and look in my child's room."

This same mother would be outraged if a neighbor, driving by, came into her house and said, "Well, I was passing by and couldn't help but open the door and look inside. What's the state of cleanliness?"

Guideline 3

KIDS NATURALLY GO THROUGH STAGES OF CLEANLINESS

As a rule of thumb, most children keep their room no cleaner than their parents keep their garage. The kids and adults both think, "Well, gee I don't live there." Often, when a child invites friends over, there may be a flurry of temporary cleanliness. Finally, concerning this whole mess issue, parents need to realize that it is difficult to keep one's total life belongings in one small space.

If a child generally shows responsibility about appearance and homework and usually likes to please the parents, don't hassle her/him about the bedroom. On the other hand, if the child is generally irresponsible, poorly motivated, or has a poor self-image (as is usually the case in poorly-motivated children), pay attention to the room and use cleanliness to build self-esteem. This attention to cleanliness has several advantages:

1. The condition of the room is easily checked.

2. It's fairly easy to come up with rewards for keeping a clean room.

3. The room can be used to build self-esteem. "Wow! How do you feel about that?"

4. The child can easily learn real world consequences. For example: "Please have your room finished by the time you eat your next meal."

There's a real world example of this in all of our lives. First we get our jobs done. Then we eat. That's the way it works for most adults.

Many parents worry that if their children have messy rooms, they will never learn to keep their homes neat as adults. However, there seems to be no real correlation between a clean room and a clean house later on in life. The real correlation is between how the parents keep their home and how the child eventually keeps his/her home.

Once more, as we always say in the philosophy of Love and Logic, the real emphasis over the long run needs to be on modeling done by the parents. Jim Fay often talks about how his father tried to teach him to pick up after himself. He did this by yelling, "You get that picked up right now! When are you ever going to learn to pick up after yourself?" Dad always made the kids clean up instead of being a good model for them.

Jim wasn't trying to learn to be a kid—he was trying to act like the big people in his life. As a result, when he grew into an adult, he picked up his things as poorly as his father and drove his wife crazy. Guess what his own kids were learning to do? I bet you can guess what Jim told his kids: "You get that picked up right now! When are you going to learn to pick up after yourselves?" It worked just as poorly for Jim as it did for his father.

Fortunately for Jim and his children, he learned some new ways of doing things that have made his life, and his kids's lives, a lot better. These are the ideas you hear in his audio cassettes and read in his books.

13

Volume 3

Fighting
Volume 3, no. 1

Childhood fights. They can be tough on both parents and children. In Evergreen, we've had extensive experience with childhood fighting through our foster care program. Many of the children come into foster care as "natural born" or well-developed fighters. We have found the following six guidelines to be effective:

Guideline 1

PROTECT ONLY IF LIFE AND LIMB ARE IN DANGER—OTHERWISE EXPECT THE CHILDREN TO HANDLE IT

The first guideline is the toughest. When we hear kids fighting, we naturally want to intervene. In some cases, if we are teachers, we have a legal responsibility to intervene whether the kids need it or not.

If possible, however, it's best to put the problem on the kids. When one kid tattles on another, a good response is, "Why are you telling me?" Or, on seeing a fight, sometimes it works to say dryly, "You guys ought to form a committee," or "Please settle it somewhere where I don't have to see or hear it."

Guideline 2

HELP CHILDREN PROBLEM-SOLVE THEIR FIGHTS

Kids need help in identifying their feelings. Were they feeling mad, sad, frustrated, or left out? First, they need to identify their feelings. Then they need to identify different ways to handle those feelings.

At this point, we can use modeling: "I know that when I'm frustrated, hitting Mr. Jackson probably wouldn't make me feel as good as handling it another way. How do you think you could handle it another way?"

Sometimes it helps youngsters when the adult asks, "Would you like to hear how other kids have handled it?"

The point is, the adult must identify with the child's feelings and then help the child work out a new action.

Guideline 3

USE "I" MESSAGES

It's much better that fighting kids understand that we are going to take care of ourselves rather than try to take care of them. Then if we do need to ask the kids to leave, not play together, etc., they are not resentful. However, they would be resentful if they thought we were doing this for their own good. If we do it for our good, they accept it. It's almost magic.

Adults giving "I" messages might say, "Fights make me nervous," or "Fights turn my bile black," or "Hey, have you two both had your rabies shots? I'm extra sensitive," or "Hey, guys, this stuff hassles my eyeballs!"

I want to stress here the importance of humor. It may be used to lighten up an otherwise heavy situation. More than that, when we can joke about something it almost always says that we have it under some control. When something is too "heavy" to be joked about, anxiety often causes us to handle the problem poorly.

Guideline 4

GIVE KIDS A COOL-OFF TIME

People of all ages need time to cool off. Then they can get back together to talk. However, a cool-off time is not a freeze out. (Those involved in marital games, take note!) After giving children the time they need to cool off, it's good to make sure they get back together and work things out. Kids usually know how long they need to cool off. If not, it helps to say, "Let's talk as soon as your voice is as soft as mine."

Guideline 5

MAKE AN INDIVIDUAL CONTRACT FOR CHANGE

The individual contract for change seldom needs to be in writing. It covers the following:

1. How did the child feel?
2. How did the child act?
3. How is the situation to be handled in the future?
4. What will be the consequence if it is not handled differently in the future?

Guideline 6

GIVE CONSEQUENCES ONLY IF A DIFFICULT CHILD HAS TROUBLE DEALING WITH A CONTRACT THAT SAYS NO FIGHTS

When giving out consequences, it is important for the adults to note, "I want to come up with something that helps you remember. I also want to come up with something you feel good about."

A therapist tells the story of Jake coming to the office with his professional foster parent. Jake had been a terror just three weeks earlier after arriving in the foster care program. Now, his fighting had almost stopped.

When the therapist asked him about this, Jake said, "Well, I hate doing all the chores. When I fight, my mom says it drains energy from the family, but when I scrub the walls, it puts energy back into the family." Jake, I might note, said this with no anger toward his foster parents. As he related this story, he looked up at his mother and smiled.

These consequences were meted out to take care of the mother, not to take care of Jake. Furthermore, his mother did not have to tell Jake what to do. She didn't say, "Stop fighting!" Such orders seldom work on children like Jake. Instead, when Jake would fight, his wonderful parent would say in a loving way, "Jake, I feel a drain coming on . . . " Jake changed quickly.

Parents and grandparents both have rights
when it comes to disciplining the kids. Read on to learn more.

Parents and Grandparents: Who's the Boss?
Volume 3, no. 2

It's summertime. Time for families to get together. At this time of year, rare and wonderful moments often take place between grandparents and their grandchildren and between grown parents and their own parents.

And throughout time, most parents have always known that they can palm their kids off on the grandparents because both grandparents and kids love it!

Unfortunately this is not always the case. Some parents choose to raise their children differently than the way they were raised—especially if they were raised with techniques different from Love and Logic.

The grandparents may not understand what is going on between parents and children. For instance, parents who espouse the Love and Logic philosophy are sad for their children rather than mad. They provide consequences for their children rather than react with anger and frustration. They substitute kindness for protectionism, concern for worry and look for ways to provide their children with responsibility. They allow for failure, knowing the price tag of failure may be affordable and their children will learn from these experiences.

When grandparents do not understand the techniques used by parents, they may become critical or accusatory: "How could you let Drew do that?" When around such older parents, the grown children often feel like children again. They may revert back to old childhood behavior patterns.

I have seen the whining and pleading routine go on between adults—even in nursing homes. Instead of two adults relating on an adult level, we find a parent-to-child relationship which is not rewarding for either person. Boiled down to its essentials, the older parent's message is: "You never do anything right. You can't even raise Drew right, so I'll have to do it!" The grown child responds with, "You never liked anything I did. And now you can't even accept the way I raise my own children!"

There are ways to handle overly critical or intrusive grandparents. Before looking at them specifically, keep in mind that the way parents treat their own parents is the way they will be treated by their own children.

In a few unhappy cases parents and children have had a downright toxic relationship. And that might not be because of anything the children are doing. Sometimes adult children are drawn to their parents like moths to a flame, forever being burnt, but forever going back, always hoping for a close relationship that will never occur. As a psychiatrist, I see this futile, sad and compulsive search frequently.

Except for a few fortunate souls, most of us will probably go through life never being totally accepted by our parents, and all the energy spent trying to make it happen will only end in more frustration.

This is an important issue that must be kept in mind before we focus on the following three techniques for working with difficult grandparents.

Be assertive about your wishes

Rather than react to the content of the grandparent's statement, it's best for parents to handle things in an assertive manner. For instance, a parent might say to her own parents, "Mom, before you comment on how I raise my children, I hope you'll first inquire about it lovingly and ask me why I am handling things the way I do. Does this sound reasonable to you?"

Let grandparents know why adult interaction takes place

Not everyone realizes that adult interaction only takes place for one of the following three reasons:

1. Adults work together to get something accomplished.

2. Adults get together because of a sense of guilt or obligation.

3. Adults get together to have fun.

Sometimes parents need to understand these reasons. "Mom and Dad, the only reason people get together on vacations is either out of a sense of obligation and guilt or to have fun together. I'm wondering if you see our times together as fun. If not, what do you see as answers? I ask this because I'm unwilling for us to relate purely out of a sense of obligation or guilt."

As we look at the content of conflict, it may be important, after an accusation or a cutting comment, to ask, "Is there any answer or response that I could give you right now that would really make you happy?"

Clarify bottom line expectations

Individuals may have different bottom line expectations of others. One bottom line request parents might make is that the grandparents do not comment negatively on parenting techniques in front of the grandchildren. Another bottom line request might be that the grandparents do not discipline the children without parental permission.

Likewise, grandparents have rights. If the children are acting like hellions, they have the right either to ask their own children to handle the grandchildren, or to ask the entire tribe to leave!

Let's also remember that the parenting techniques used today are often very different than those used by the grandparents. Educating the grandparents in the art of Love and Logic is a kind and thoughtful act which often pays high dividends.

This can easily be done by saying, "Mom and Dad, I'd like you to hear about my techniques from Foster Cline and Jim Fay on this audio cassette so that you'll understand why I handle my kids the way I do."

Grandparents find the audio cassette, *Helicopters, Drill Sergeants and Consultants,* to be both entertaining and informative. They often want to discuss the tape's contents. New understandings are created.

The guidelines for handling grandparents are somewhat similar to the guidelines for handling children. Be assertive. Take care of yourself in a loving way. Concentrate on problem-solving rather than frustration and anger. Provide consequences if necessary.

The next article explores how to reduce stress on the homefront.

~つ

An Overview of Stress in the Family
Volume 9, no. 3

It has been said that money, sex, and kids—just those three subjects—are the cause of all stress in a family. Maybe. But then again, what else is there?

Some people can anticipate stress about every seven years. It seems to come in cycles similar to the seven-year itch. When kids have trouble in the seventh grade, they sometimes have trouble again seven years later in the second year of college. Marriages seem to experience difficulties around multiples of seven: seven years, fourteen years, twenty-one years.

In reality, it's more fruitful to look at stress by examining its underlying causes. We all have stressful events in our lives, but not everyone gets "stressed out."

Personality problem or communication problem?

If a person is married to someone who appears irritable, angry, and "stressed out," the underlying problem could be either 1) a communication problem or 2) an outright personality problem.

Here are a couple of "litmus test" questions. If the answers are positive, then we are dealing with a personality problem. First, we must ask whether the stressed out person would be hard to live with no matter what the stress. Second, would he or she be stressed out no matter who they lived with?

If the answer is "yes," then the individual needs help. Personality problems can often be effectively helped with therapy or counseling. However, if this individual does not want help, then it becomes our problem. Then we need help.

The best self-help groups emphasize that we take good care of ourselves in the face of negative and difficult partners. Perhaps the model group is Al-Anon. Although our basic principles may not be alcohol related, the principles of Al-Anon work and teach everyone to cope effectively in a wide variety of difficult situations.

Self-image

Poor self-image is another personality trait that can lead a person to feeling "stressed out." When people with a poor self-image make a mistake, they come down hard on themselves with statements like, "I goofed again;" "When will I ever learn?" or "I'm no good."

Contrast this to what people with a high self-image say when they make a mistake: "Another learning experience! I'll sure learn from this one!" At the very least, people with a high self-image tend to realize that much of the problem may lie in the situation and not in themselves. There is therefore much less self-blame.

Tips for solving communication issues

Fortunately, communication issues lie at the root of a great deal of family stress. I say "fortunately" because communication issues are usually easier to handle than personality problems. Generally, communication issues require only education, not therapy, and most of us are certainly capable of being educated.

The use of "I" messages is emphasized in all communication education. "I" messages tell the other person where we stand, rather than where they need to go.

"I" messages tend to be assertive rather than aggressive. Instead of telling the kids to "be quiet," a wise parent says, "I'd appreciate less noise, please . . . thank you," in a tone of voice that lovingly assumes compliance.

Using an "I" message, this spouse says, "Dear, it would help me if you'd leave your problems at work. I know that's hard to do, but bringing them home stresses me out." Such a statement is less likely to cause stress than saying, "Hey, dear, don't take your work problems out on me!"

Studies conducted in Evergreen show that a sense of humor, in and of itself, tends to help many individuals cope with stressful situations.

Individuals who communicate well automatically tend to separate all problems into "mine and the other guy's." In simplest terms, if we get involved in problems that affect us directly, we tend to be more effective and less "stressed out." We care about problems other people may have; however, we need to work on our own! In other words, we should have "global concern" and "local involvement."

Taking care of our own problems allows us more easily to say to our child, "Gee, honey, I hope you figure it out." Parents who separate problems easily are less likely to say, "Now what do I do?" when looking at their children's problems.

Mothers who tend to ask, "Now what do I do?" have children who respond with, "I don't know, but I hope you figure it out, Mom!"

Generally speaking, when we help another person without his permission, he ends up not only ungrateful, but downright resentful! Then we are surprised, saying, "Gee, I was only trying to help!"

There is a growing awareness of the need for good communication techniques in both business and families. From business seminars to church groups to non-credit classes, there are a number of ways to learn communication skills no matter where you live. These classes emphasize communication skills such as assertive, non-aggressive statements that decrease misunderstanding and stress levels.

Stress is almost never constant. We are always experiencing either more or less of it. Life throws waves of stressful situations at us, then troughs of peaceful periods. To cope with the periods of stress that are certainly ahead for all of us, we need to look at our own family patterns and communication issues in a preventive way during the non-stressful periods when we are relaxed.

What's your "hassle quota?"
Foster presents this intriguing concept in the next article.

ル゛

Hassles: What You Get May Be What You Expect
Volume 3, no. 4

We all have different "hassle quotas." This quota is a measure of what we expect to put up with in life. A "hassle quota" affects what we expect from our spouses and what we expect from our children. The higher our hassle quota, the more negative behavior we tolerate.

For instance, consider the different hassle quotas of two young mothers with 15-month-old infants. Both of their babies have tried crying during the night. Mom Number One has a high hassle quota. "What can you do! You just can't leave them in their bed crying for half-an-hour. I'm getting no sleep at night," she says. This mother is unconsciously saying to her 15-month-old, "Oh, what a hassle life is!"

Mom Number Two, who enjoys a low hassle quota, says, "I found that when I didn't get up when Katherine cried, she started sleeping through the night." This mom does not expect life to be a constant hassle.

Parents with a high hassle quota move things out of an infant's reach—to avoid a possible "hassle" in their home. These same parents involve themselves in their child's fights—anticipating the worst while depriving the child of learning experiences. The hassle quota has a powerful but unseen influence on everyone!

Doing or "done-in"
People with a high hassle quota always feel that things are "done" to them. They give strong covert messages that the child is in control of the parents. Such parents might say, "You'll be the death of me!"

Of course, depending on the parent/child relationship, the child might answer back, "Good," or "That's sorta bad," or "I might even miss you some."

I recently saw a young mother named Patty who let her own mother undermine her relationship with her own daughter. The grandmother gave Patty's daughter all kinds of extravagant gifts and allowed the youngster to be disrespectful. Patty has felt hassled by her mother all of her life. Now she is allowing her daughter to hassle her. What's more, she expects her daughter and mother to gang up on her. Of course, they comply with her expectations.

Everyone reading this article has expectations about hassles. The more hassles we expect, the lower our expectations of others. Individuals with a high hassle quota expect their children to be a hassle at both school and at home. They say, "Isn't that just the way things are?"

Unfortunately, for these parents, the answer is "yes."

14

Volume 4

Facing Our Own Problems, Allowing Kids to Face Theirs
Volume 4, no. 1

There are several practical benefits of figuring out who really owns a problem. In fact, difficulties in figuring out, "Whose problem is this?" keep children's shrinks in business! When parents don't figure out who has the problem, the result is an irresponsible child.

"Units of concern" is a useful concept that can help parents sort out who owns the problem. Every problem has a given number of units of concern. And you can bet nobody wants to carry those units of concern around—least of all the child causing the problem!

Most kids would prefer that their teachers and parents carry these units. If the parent insists on worrying about whether a child does his/her homework, for example, then the child is free to drop that concern.

Parents who carry their children's concerns are about as effective as if they were trying to solve another nation's problems. Suppose for a moment that tonight's evening news features a green Martian. With his antennas waving and yellow eyes bulging, he might declare, "Earthlings, you are a very warlike species! You could wipe each other out! From now on, we're not going to let you hurt each other. We're going to step in! The missiles of any nation being fired at another nation will immediately be destroyed. We're doing this because we love you!"

Can you imagine the response? You bet. Within 15 minutes, both the United States and Russia would be shooting at the Martians, who would end up saying, "Well, we were only trying to help!" Yet it never helps and it never works to take on someone else's problem.

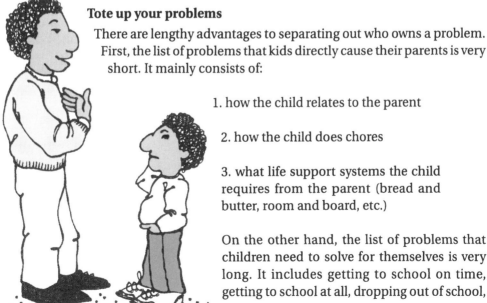

Tote up your problems

There are lengthy advantages to separating out who owns a problem. First, the list of problems that kids directly cause their parents is very short. It mainly consists of:

1. how the child relates to the parent

2. how the child does chores

3. what life support systems the child requires from the parent (bread and butter, room and board, etc.)

On the other hand, the list of problems that children need to solve for themselves is very long. It includes getting to school on time, getting to school at all, dropping out of school, being hassled by friends, hassling friends, harassing teachers, being harassed by teachers, and more. Frankly, it's an unending list. Parents who get involved in their children's problems can keep themselves busy for a lifetime!

Why go for someone else's hassle?

Unconscious benefits often prompt parents to ignore the issue of "who owns the problem." These unconscious "pluses" for seizing someone else's problem might include scenarios such as when parents get involved in their children's problems, it may hold a rickety marriage together. I remember a father who lamented, "After the kids left home, my wife and I had nothing to talk or fight about!"

Second, getting involved in another persons's problems definitely gives life a purpose. Unconsciously, we tell ourselves we could successfully handle the problem if only we were in the driver's seat!

On the other hand, if we work on our own problems but run into trouble, we fear we'll see ourselves as a failure. So, if we're a fat parent, it's easier to fret about what our kids eat rather than what we eat.

Third, never figuring out "Whose problem is it?" allows individuals to carry a "hassle" script. Some people feel that everything is a problem. For this to hold true, such people need to be involved in problems virtually all of the time.

When anyone around them has a problem, these harried people think, "Now what will I do?" rather than asking the healthy question, "Now what are you going to do?"

If everyone figured out, "Who really owns this problem?" most problems between nations would be solved. Most battles on the homefront would work themselves out. Would we be bored!

Do you and your spouse have different views on parenting?
If so, you'll want to read on . . .

ᕦ

When Parents Differ: On Presenting a United Front
Volume 4, no. 2

Differences in parenting techniques are normal

Almost all couples disagree on some aspect of parenting. Whew! That's nice to know, isn't it? Yet in the thick of a three-way conflict—pitting parent against parent against child—a parent can sometimes feel totally isolated and bewildered.

When you think about it, disagreement is natural and totally human. We usually don't marry someone who is identical to us; instead we marry someone who complements us. By definition, complementary means different! If the differences in beliefs between two people are not extreme, it is quite all right to disagree.

As adults, our lives are spent around bosses who differ from each other. Some bosses allow employees to be two or three minutes late while some do not. Some bosses allow their employees great latitude in doing their jobs; some do not. Generally, individuals adjust to different bosses.

Likewise, children adjust to parents who differ. They know which parent to go to for money, which parent to go to for freedom, and which parent to go to for affection. As parents, we can help our children work within the family system so that everyone knows who said what to whom and when so that our children are not tempted to do this:

Tara: "Mom, can I go to Jenny's?"

Mom: "No."

Tara: "Mom! It's OK with Dad if it's OK with you."

Mom: "Really? Well, I don't think you should go."

Tara: "But Mom!"

Mom: "All right. If Dad said it's OK, it's OK with me."

Tara: "Dad, Mom said if it's OK with you, I can go to Jenny's."

Dad: "If it's OK with your mom, it's OK with me."

Let your children know early on that they must always accept the answer they get first from either parent. (Therefore, it is important that they ask the proper parent the proper question!) Children are not allowed to ask the same question of both parents.

Hiding differences is usually not effective

It's usually acceptable for parents to acknowledge their differences in front of the children. However, it's not acceptable to argue about those differences in front of them.

It's fine for Dad to say, "Hey, this is the way your mother wants this done, and I'm going to back her up on it." Thus, he is saying, "I'm different, but accepting of your mom." He is modeling the correct attitude. The children then say to themselves, "I may not like what Mom is saying, but I'm going to do it her way."

With some children, a united front is more essential

When children have behavior or personality problems, it becomes very important for parents to present a united front. Difficult children tend to manipulate and drive wedges between adults who disagree. In fact, disturbed children hope the adults in their environment disagree!

Usually these children will bad-mouth teachers to the parents, bad-mouth parents to the teachers, and bad-mouth one parent to the other. The best way to handle such complaints is to say to the child, "If you have something negative to say about your mom, tell her. Don't tell me—I don't want to hear it." Likewise, parents need to say to such children,"If you have problems with your teacher, talk to her about it."

Self-help

When disagreements about parenting become a frequent issue, it helps to take a closer look. Make a three-part list of concerns and disagreements. Write down:

Specifically what the child does to incite disagreement

How each parent feels about the behavior

How each parent tends to discipline the behavior

Go over the issues thoroughly and decide what each parent can and cannot live with in terms of behavior and approaches to discipline. There will be some issues that parents need to compromise on. On difficult issues, the disagreeing parent might back up the other parent while discussions continue. Writing things out can effectively clear the air in many cases.

Ask a friend or counselor

When self-help doesn't work, seek outside help. If you come prepared, one good solid hour of counseling can go a long way. Take your list of concerns and disagreements and stick to them until they're mediated to everyone's satisfaction.

It's not always necessary to get professional feedback. Parents can help parents. Sometimes when we're having a hard time, it's better to seek advice from parents who are not experiencing difficultly. Often, parents who have worked their way through a certain stage your child is now in can be particularly informative. They may have found an effective technique you have yet to discover.

Most people are only too happy to help out. You might say, "You know, John and Joyce are really great kids. Sometimes we wish our kids acted like they do. Jamie has started to back talk us, and we'd like your thoughts on how you handle that. Would you like to come over for coffee sometime so we can talk?"

Join the human race

Parents are often overly strict because they are frustrated and don't know what to do next. When a child is "grounded for 100 years," or grounded more than he/she is free, this almost always indicates parental frustration and lack of education over a specific issue.

Parents "at the end of their rope" tend to become ineffective. Then disagreements begin. Sometimes parents feel so ineffective that they become defensive. They may say or think, "No one else can tell me how to my raise my kid."

We all have moments of frustration with our children. We sometimes need an outside opinion. No big deal. Good parent education—whether it is self-taught, group, private counseling, or peer counseling—can inevitably decrease disagreements between parents and almost always enhance a couple's relationship as well.

Learn how to share the burden of worry with your children in Foster's next article.

~๑

Techniques for Effective Worry
Volume 4, no. 3

Why worry about worry? Some people stave off depression through continual worry. Without realizing it, worry gives them something to do! Haven't we all known parents who worried about how their teens are doing in school, only to have the youngster leave home and do well? Are the folks happy? Not necessarily.

Many individuals suffer acute depression once the object of their worry disappears, be it a cantankerous spouse or an angry teenager. This concept is succinctly written in the sign above the bar room mirror: "I'm too busy to have my nervous breakdown right now. I'll have it later when things slow down and I can enjoy it."

Many of us simply need to look at ourselves and accept that we may be chronic worriers. Paradoxically, once this acceptance takes place, we worry less. At any rate, we're not worried about our worries, so that in itself calms the situation somewhat. Change your mindset—worry less about the children

Parents who worry the most about their children tend to be those who say to themselves, "Now what do I do?" This is much less effective than parents who have mindsets that allow them to say to the children, "What a bummer! Now what will you do?"

The latter group of parents tends to have children who worry about themselves. Consequently, the parents tend to worry less! Happy parents arrange situations so that their children do the worrying. Conversations with their children go something like this:

Dad: "John, I heard what happened at school today. I'll bet you're unhappy. What in the world are you going to do now?"

John: "I don't know!"

Dad: "Well, if I were in your shoes and had your problems, and didn't know what I was going to do, I know I'd really be upset. No wonder you're so down!"

If the child wasn't properly worried before this conversation, he certainly will be afterwards!

Worry about the right things

It is generally not practical to worry about what our children are doing when they are away from us. However, it is generally effective to express our concern about how they think when they are with us.

Parents who worry about the things their children are doing when they're away often tend to be mad when the children are with them. Such parents might say, "I heard about all the drinking that went on at that party! The way you behave really makes me mad!" Such statements generally do not bring about change in a child, but instead encourage rebellion.

On the other hand, parents who say, "Hey, Jason. I heard about the party you were at the other night. Considering the things that you think are fun, I'm sometimes concerned about your thinking. I really hope things work out well for you. Sometimes, Jason, I look at you and think, 'Boy, am I glad that I'm not Jason.' But you know how it is, everyone to their own thing. But I'm still concerned about your thinking."

When parents tell a child, "I'm concerned about your thinking," the adult is really covertly saying, "I know there's nothing I can do, and it is your problem." Parents who get angry at children for what they have done are really saying, "What can I do about you?" And the children in their own way answer back, "I hope you figure something out." Hence, the children tend to worry less while the parents worry more.

Common needless worries

Many parents worry about their teens, when in reality they need to trust the parenting they provided the child through age 11. Generally, if children are loving and achievement-oriented through this age, they need lots of love but fewer limits thereafter. Such children build on the good value systems they learn in elementary school and usually do well. When parents "crack down" on basically good kids, it tends to make them more rebellious.

Parents can usually say to these children, "Honey it's your life and I hope things go well for you. Knowing you, they probably will!"

Life consists of phases. When our children are having problems with their friends in fifth grade, we can assure them that this stage will pass. Sometimes parents lose sight of the fact that their parenting difficulties or problems are simply another stage. This too shall pass.

Hope for mistakes—don't worry about them

Finally, I see some parents worried about things they should hope take place! For instance, it's great when a child who lives less than six miles from school gets kicked off the bus for calling the driver a name. How wonderful! Usually the child has to walk to school for a week.

Boy do they learn! Calling the bus driver a name is definitely tacky but does not fall in the same category as someone at age 30 calling their employer an obscene name—resulting in a lost job.

Wise parents hope that their toddler checks out a hot object by touching it lightly. This hurts the child, and, of course, that is sad. However, it does not fall into the same league as checking out the whirling blades of a lawn mower at age seven. It's best that children get most of their hard knocks in life in toddlerhood, so that they'll learn and suffer less in mid-childhood and adolescence.

Wise parents hope their children make a lot of mistakes because they can then say to them, "Well, you're a chip off the old block. I hope you make lots of mistakes, because I know you will learn from them! You're just like me!"

Foster presents five guidelines for raising responsible teens in the next article.

↜つ

Five Guidelines for Handling Teenagers
Volume 4, no. 4

Guideline 1
GIVE AS MANY RULES AS ABSOLUTELY NECESSARY, BUT AS FEW AS POSSIBLE
It's common for parents to make too many rules for teenagers. Children usually need fewer, not more rules as they grow older.

I'll never forget an unhappy 16-year-old who sat crying in my office. As she wiped away her tears, she wailed, "When I was a little girl, I didn't have to tell my parents where I was if I happened to be late for dinner. I didn't have to tell them what I was doing every minute. It's not my fault I grew boobs, Dr. Cline. Every girl grows boobs!"

In her own adolescent way, this young woman was saying that her parents were making an all-too-common mistake. When she curved out, they clamped down!

Guideline 2
GIVE ONLY THOSE RULES AND ORDERS THAT CHILDREN WILL FOLLOW
The quickest way for parents to lose the respect of their children is to give them orders they will not follow. For instance, when children are grounded, they may retaliate by sneaking out the window or by categorically refusing to follow the order.

Generally speaking, grounding works poorly for children and spouses. It didn't even work for God! When he grounded the folks in the desert for 40 years, they rebelled. Usually, the only rules that parents can "force" an adolescent to follow are rules that directly affect the parents.

People tend to disregard rules that are for their own good. Thus, a rule that a teen cannot smoke marijuana may be not followed. However, a rule that prohibits marijuana on the premises will probably be effective. Likewise, we cannot necessarily set rules about our adolescent's behavior with a teacher or coach; however, we can certainly insist that he/she show us respect!

Guideline 3

KEEP LINES OF COMMUNICATION OPEN

Sounds fairly simple, but it's hard to do! If we talk to our children as a therapist talks to kids, they'll most likely open up.

In fact, many people pay $100 an hour to talk with a therapist. Evidently they're worth it. When parents are having trouble with their teens, things often straighten out with the help of a good therapist. Just what do these therapists actually do?

First, the therapist listens attentively, paraphrases what the child says and makes absolutely certain that he/she understands the child's point of view.

Second, since the therapist usually cannot force the child to do anything, he/she seldom gives orders.

Third, the therapist almost always offers his/her advice and opinions and clearly labels them as such. The child understands that he/she is always responsible for decision-making and consequences.

Fourth, the therapist conveys an unqualified, positive message. That is, in his/her actions, the therapist says, "I may not think what you're doing is great, but as a person, you're all right."

These four ways of talking with adolescents are actually very simple. But they may go against the grain and be hard for parents to carry out.

Nevertheless, experience shows that adults who are the best consultants are also the best parents. Furthermore, their children are actually friendly with them!

Too often a parent looks at his/her child with worry and concern when the correct response should be interest and curiosity. It's much more fruitful to try to understand an adolescent's life than to try to control it. Breakfasts at the pancake house and riding in the car are excellent times to talk things over if the parent shows true interest, curiosity, and caring.

Guideline 4

ENCOURAGE ADOLESCENTS TO SHOW THEIR AUTONOMY BY BEING DIFFERENT

Adolescents like to be different. They like being unique. Healthy adolescents act in unique but non-destructive ways. Ten years ago, long hair was the non-destructive way of expression. Today, long hair is out. The issue for boys is now an earring.

Wearing an earring is non-destructive. Some parents are as upset about the earring as parents were upset ten years ago about long hair. This is very gratifying to the adolescent, who is trying for some type of parental disapproval just to make sure he is really different from his parents.

As a rule of thumb, changes in dress are generally not self-destructive. In fact, when applying for a job that requires conventional dress, almost all responsible adolescents will follow the dress codes—unless their parents are trying to force them to follow the guidelines.

Appearance changes, such as an earring or slightly weird hair style, are definitely in and of themselves not a problem. If the child is responsible, these changes make no difference. On the other hand, if the child is basically irresponsible, acts out, and is negative and angry, parents have a lot more important things to worry about than superficial appearance! Either way, appearance simply is not that important.

Guideline 5

KEEP LIFE CONSEQUENTIAL FOR THE ADOLESCENT

Wise parents arrange things so that problem behavior always affects the adolescent directly and not the parents. Therefore, parents are able to show sorrow and sadness for the teen rather than anger and frustration. Common examples include:

1. Wise parents pay for "good guy" auto insurance. If the teen receives a ticket, poor grades, or engages in other behavior that results in an increase in insurance rates, the adolescent pays the different rate increase. The parents says, "What a bummer—your insurance is going to shoot through the ceiling."

2. If the adolescent is slightly irresponsible and may have trouble in college, wise parents never pay the full tuition. The teen is required to come up with some percentage of matching funds. Or, the parents will only reimburse her for a semester successfully completed. Therefore, if a youngster flunks, she flunks on her own money.

3. If an adolescent engages in tacky, expensive behavior, such as marring the furniture or ruining the lawn with car tracks, wise parents take money out of the youngster's college fund or inheritance. They let him know that, whether or not he actually has the money at the moment, he is paying for costs that he incurs.

4. Wise parents let their children know that they will never pay attorney fees. Wise parents let their children know that, should they engage in illegal behavior, obtaining a public defender may be a hassle. Wise parents let their children know that, should they ever be in detention, they will send them a care package. Even a teen in detention deserves a box of goodies! However, wise parents will not be there to bail their child out.

15

Volume 5

Learning Disorders: No Easy Answers
Volume 5, no. 1

As many as two children in ten are diagnosed with a learning disorder, perceptual motor problem, and/or dyslexia. These common terms are used to describe a child who is 1) normally intelligent and 2) has learning problems—usually academic learning.

Learning disorders almost never exist in isolation. Most children have a combination of learning disorders, behavioral problems, and/or attitude problems towards school. Many children may also have associated neurologic "soft signs" or indications of definite neurologic (brain) dysfunction.

The importance of an accurate diagnosis

Simply stating that a child has a learning disorder or dyslexia is not very specific. It is like diagnosing a person who walks abnormally as having a limp.

When we diagnose "limp," we really don't know the reason for the problem and therefore can't be very helpful to the individual. Perhaps the person had a hip replacement. Maybe she has a problem with her knees. Or, did he perhaps drop a hammer on his toe? All these things can cause a limp.

Therefore, when a child has a learning problem, the specifics of the problem need to be determined before a solution can be reached. Many learning problems can be cured or helped; others need to be coped with or compensated for. Curing and coping are very different responses and are only possible after correct diagnosis.

Too often parents encounter a great deal of needless agony, wheel-spinning and financial outlay when they try to fix a problem that:

1. will disappear with time anyway
2. cannot be fixed
3. is not even the basic problem

How to diagnose a learning disorder

There are two ways to diagnose a learning disorder. The first and most important way is by obtaining an accurate history:

Were there birth or pregnancy problems?
When did the child master his/her milestones, such as crawling, walking, sitting alone, feeding him/herself, talking, etc.?
Did the mother or father or do the siblings have any problems in school?

The second diagnostic tool is the tests designed to help clarify a learning disorder. The testing concepts consist of a fairly simple three-step process: 1) How does the perception get into the brain? 2) How are these perceptions worked with in the brain? 3) How does the individual express his/her perceptions?

Helpful tests include:

- Tests of sensory competence, including vision and hearing tests. (These should be done first. Many children diagnosed with a learning disorder are actually partially deaf.)
- A general intelligence test—the WISC-R.
- Tests of visual and auditory integration and synthesis processing.
- Tests of both fine and gross motor output function.

What to do about learning disorders

What one does about the problem is based upon an accurate diagnosis. However, there are some generalities worth stating:

1. No matter what the problem, maintaining a high self-image is essential. Children must feel good about themselves while recognizing their learning problems.

Wise parents and educators focus on building the child's own strengths rather than correcting their weaknesses. Often this focus on strengths takes place in non-academic or extracurricular areas.

2. Children may outgrow learning disorders. For example, a six-to-ten-year-old, particularly a boy, may have been "slow" in milestone development. His handwriting is messy, he is poor in drawing, and he has problems in math and spelling. However, if he now walks and talks without residual problems and has a normal vocabulary, he will probably outgrow most of his problems in early adolescence.

It is the adult's task to help such children feel good about themselves while they work on their academic problems in elementary and early junior high school.

3. If a learning disorder is accompanied by Attention Deficit Disorder (ADD), ritalin or other medications may be of great help. (ADD is a whole different topic.)

4. If a child is to be "specially remediated" in the education system, the size of the class, the behavior of the other children, and the ability of the teacher to respond to the child as a unique individual are the three factors most important to the child's success.

5. Tutoring by a good teacher can be of great help only if a child buys into the program.

Making Chores No Chores
Volume 5, no. 2

When handled correctly, chores help build a child's self-image and sense of self-worth while providing feelings of competence and responsibility.

However, when parents handle chores incorrectly, a child experiences the opposite—poor self-esteem, a lack of motivation, and a decreased sense of responsibility. These negative factors take place mainly when parents and children fight about chores.

At first, the great triad—fun, getting things done, and the parents—are happily intertwined in a toddler's mind as she helps the parents make beds or rake leaves. This early childhood help, is, of course, no help at all. The child is simply modeling the parents and having some fun at the same time.

The Mary Poppins song, "A Spoonful of Sugar," provides us with a good example of pairing work and fun in early childhood.

As parents, we can be assured that children have no more fun getting their jobs done than we have getting our own jobs completed. As a physician, I model having fun doing my office work at home. In fact, I call it "my homework" and always make sure I get it done in front of the kids. Then I play!

It's important for children to know what they need to do and when the job is expected to be completed. It is unfair to suddenly come up with new and unexpected jobs. We do not want to be an, "Oh, by the way, will you also please . . . " type of parent. For some parents, it's as if the sight of their child reminds them of jobs that need to be done.

An effective way for parents to state when a job needs to be completed is the following: "Honey, I would like your room cleaned before you leave it this weekend," or "I would like the dishes and homework completed before you watch TV," or "I would like the garage cleaned before your next meal."

Notice that it is best to give a child a weekend job, with the understanding that when he has completed the job, he has the rest of the weekend off.

This is more effective than saying, "We are working on chores this Saturday morning." Kids, like adults, may simply put in their time and not get much accomplished.

When there are a number of chores to do, and more than one child, it's best to let the children divide up the jobs and set timelines for their completion. The less the parents are involved in chores, the better!

When children are allowed to assign the chores for the week, one child may end up being taken advantage of. It won't be long before the children rectify the situation among themselves. But, authorities differ on whether children should be paid for chores or whether their allowance should be contingent on the completion of chores.

My own feeling is that a child's usual chores—dishes, laundry, cleaning the garage and carrying out the trash—may be considered his payment for being part of the family.

Special large projects—window cleaning, car washing, and other non-routine jobs—definitely deserve pay and should be used to help children both earn and learn the value of money.

Finally, it helps develop better parent/child and sibling relationships if the oldest child is not always expected to babysit the younger kids without being paid.

Now let's look at handling refusals to do chores. Generally, chronic problems centered around completing chores should be discussed when the problem is not taking place and when both parent and child are in a good mood.

The beauty of a chronic problem is that we can wait until the very best time to solve it. No sense rushing into it—it will always come up again!

This mother has picked a time of mutual good feelings and calmness to discuss a chronic problem—Cindy's refusal to complete her chores in a timely manner.

Mom: "Honey, is this a good time to talk a minute?"

Cindy: "Sure."

Mom: "I'd like to discuss you getting the dishes done."

Cindy: "Oh—I know, but I have so much to do . . . "

Mom: "I know you are really busy, honey. What do you think is the answer?"

Cindy: "I don't know . . . (silence) I know I should get them done, but I don't have time sometimes when I get home late from piano lessons and Scouts."

Mom: "I know. What would you think about getting them done in the morning?"

Cindy: "You mean I could leave them at night?"

Mom: "As long as the dishes are done and the kitchen is clean by the time you leave for school, I think it would be OK with me."

Cindy: "You mean I couldn't leave for school before the kitchen was clean?"

Mom: "What do you think?"

Talking about chores involves, as always, exploring the child's feelings, and setting consequences, mainly by asking questions. Consequences might include getting the child up at midnight if the chore is not done by the end of the day as agreed; paying another sibling to do the job; paying ourselves as parents to do the child's job; paying an outsider to do the job; or, taking the other children on a fun outing while the leaving the child who refuses to do the chores at home to think.

In the next article, Foster presents
the "Basic German Shepherd" method of handling toddlers.

Handling Toddlers
Volume 5, no. 3

Happy toddlers become happy adolescents. Likewise, unhappy and out-of-control toddlers become tomorrow's delinquents.

These are pretty strong statements. Nevertheless, research has shown them to be true. Since the 1930s, psychological researchers have emphasized the importance of early childhood. Therefore, the way parents treat their toddlers is of utmost importance.

Toddlerhood is the adolescence of early childhood, which matures and ends when a child is around age four. Adolescence itself can be compared to toddlerhood. In fact, at Evergreen Consultants, we coined the phrase, "Adolescents are toddlers with hormones and wheels."

Because both toddlers and adolescents are involved in issues that revolve around autonomy and identity, the way toddlers and their parents cope with these issues will be reflected in adolescence a short 10 or 12 years down the road.

Toddlerhood is the time when a child must learn parental control and "internalize" that control so it later manifests as self-control. What are the important aspects of self-control? Understanding these aspects will help us know how to respond lovingly when a little child needs parental control.

Good self-control is consistent. It does no good to give up alcohol, cigarettes, or food one day and relapse the next! Self-control is loving and firm. We control ourselves because we want to. It is ideally not harsh and punitive, but loving, firm and resolved.

If we do something because we "ought to" or "should," we may end up rebelling against ourselves. If, on the other hand, we do something because we really want to, we are much less likely to fight ourselves.

Now we have it! As parents, we want to give our children responses from the outside that they will later live with from the inside. Therefore, parents must be consistent, loving, firm, resolved, and non-punitive.

What's the difference between "firm" and "punitive?" Firm means we may occasionally swat a child if necessary to emphasize a point, but we in no way enjoy it. We swat a child in our desire to help the toddler think, learn, and remember—we don't hit her because we are "mad."

Actually, children need very little swatting. This brings us to the discussion on "Basic German Shepherd"—something a child must learn in early toddlerhood and late infancy. As a matter of fact, the elements of Basic German Shepherd are often learned when the child is put back into the crib, even before the child can walk.

At about 9 months, the infant passes the family dog in basic intelligence. At 11 through 13 months, when infants learn to walk, they are old enough to learn Basic German Shepherd—come, sit, no, go, stay.

Parents can never make an infant quit crying. Nor should they try to make the toddler quit being bothersome, quit sucking his thumb, or quit whining. However, the parents must and should control a situation when the child acts very obnoxious. This is when it's important that the child learn Basic German Shepherd.

Basic German Shepherd should be learned by 15 to 18 months at the latest. The child learns, when lovingly isolated, that there is a limit to the annoyance she can inflict on her parents.

When a child is acting annoyingly, or controllingly, either through whining or crying, the parents puts the child on his "red-hot bench" and tells the toddler to stay. At 12 or 13 months, the child will stay put and wail loudly if the parents act as if they mean business. Loud, angry wailing is the children's way of saying, "I hate doing it my mom's way, but I'm doing it."

Infants must first be taught to sit and stay in the same room as their parents. This is hard on the parents' ears, but necessary, since the chid will try to get up, come back and torment the parents. Now the parent must say loudly in an "I mean business" tone, "I SAID STAY!"

This is said in almost the exact same tone of voice one would use with a beloved pet. It is no-nonsense with the expectation that the child will obey. If the infant gets up, the parent is extremely firm about setting the child back down and repeating strongly, "I said stay!"

Some people might think a 13– to 16-month-old child is too young to learn Basic German Shepherd. However, we assure you that the normal child's receptive language is well-enough developed to know what the parent is saying and expects. In fact, if young children are allowed to annoy their parents unmercifully, it almost always increases their poor self-image!

There are three possible mistakes parents can make when teaching Basic German Shepherd. The first occurs when parents are too tough. Little kids are at times no fun. Aren't we all?

If our own parents were too strict, there is a danger that Basic German Shepherd could be overused. Everyone has a right to be crabby and moody at times, receive a little understanding and even be catered to a little.

Second, parents can be too lenient by not telling the child to go sit on the steps or bench soon enough. If parents grew up in a dysfunctional family themselves, they may put up with too much malarkey and hassle before telling the toddler goodbye for a while.

This is because, on an unconscious level, the parents expect life to be a hassle, and so raise kids who hassle them as much as they did their own parents. Many parents, in whining and pleading with their children, turn the children into people as obnoxious as their own parents.

In addition to being either too lenient or too strict, the third mistake a parent makes is confusing anger with firmness. A firm person may be loud and may even use a little physical pressure. However he does not yell and scream and never becomes frustrated.

A few last words on the use of a swat

A swat is only used to reinforce "go" and "stay," for once a toddler stays put, she is internalizing good control. A properly delivered swat is administered only with an open hand, on the rear, in an "I mean business and I'm in control" way.

In reality, if a parent loses control and spanks a child, the child is in control. The child also feels angry, resentful, and punitive. Unfortunately, that's the parent the child internalizes. Then the child will grow to believe,"When I'm angry, I lose control and give it to someone else" (and probably feel guilty afterward).

Learn the unique and specific ways
our children think in Foster's next article.

کرو

How Do Children Really Think?
Volume 5, no. 4

Something special happens to our children in their early teens. Something almost magical. They really begin to think!

When our children are in elementary school, they sometimes think they think. Even parents sometimes think their kids think. But the truth is that elementary school thinking should not be confused with adult thinking—it is truly immature and different than the thinking of most adults.

The great Swiss psychologist Jean Piaget studied the development of thinking in children. Paradoxically, his findings are often mentioned, and even more often ignored, by educational experts.

Piaget said all children go through maturational shifts in their ability to think, and that these shifts cannot be hurried or slowed by the efforts of parents or the educational system. They just automatically occur as a result of growing up.

So much for those of us who want to hurry our children's development by giving them special educational programs. They may be able to learn more, but they won't think more maturely.

Piaget called mature thinking "formal operations." He called elementary school and early junior high thinking "concrete operations." The difference in these two types of thinking lies at the heart of many parent/child misunderstandings.

Let's examine some very important issues. When our children attain "formal operations" sometime in late junior high or high school, the way they relate to parents may suddenly change:

   ♦ No longer do children bore parents with endless recitations of minute details about movies, such as, "Then he goes . . . then she goes . . . then he goes . . . etc."

   ♦ For the first time, our children understand analogies and parables. They understand sayings such as "People in glass houses shouldn't throw stones," or "Still waters run deep."

   ♦ Children understand the meaning of political cartoons on a much deeper level than just the humor of a big nose or the caricature of a public figure.

   ♦ They quit asking stupid questions to which the answer is obvious to any thinking person. Along with this, they quit complaining, "I don't get it," to what appears to adults to be a simple concept.

   ♦ They can wonder, deeply, whether the means justifies the end.

   ♦ They no longer automatically buy into their parents' value system just because they love their parents!

   ♦ They are able to analyze their parents' behavior and comment on it from a more objective perspective!

These changes can affect family relationships. When children are young, parents can yell at the kids about their mistakes, becoming overwrought and overbearing. The children react by believing what the parents say, and their self-image is lowered.

For instance, in early junior high school or even earlier, little Jason leaves a screwdriver on the lawn. His dad comes apart saying, "When will you ever learn to pick up after yourself? You act like you have no brains at all! How many times do I have to tell you to put stuff away? Why don't you grow up! Don't you do anything right?"

Jason, a seventh grader, knows simply that he's a bad kid, slow to learn, and irresponsible. He shuffles away feeling very bad about himself.

In ninth grade, Jason might rely, "You know what, Dad. You yell over all the little stuff and blow it yourself on the important issues. Don't have a cow (adolescentese for 'cool it')!"

Now his dad might yell back, "Where'd you learn to talk like that?"

Jason himself doesn't know. It's not the result of tacky peer relationships; it's God's gift as the child moves into "formal operations."

As kids move into formal operations and analyze their parents' behavior, they often suddenly show their newly-formed abilities in angry outbursts and sharp retorts.

Parents, often taken aback, feel the child is being disrespectful. But the fact is, the child is just being honest. Maybe for the first time, children are saying things to the parent that everyone at the work place really wants to say, but doesn't.

More importantly, perhaps, children are first able to judge truly whether they can handle a difficult situation. In fact, for the first time, the child's judgment on issues that affect his own life may truly be better than his parents.

What a change! And all this happens slowly and quietly over a period of about six months. No bells, No whistles. No warning.

When parents have raised basically responsible kids, this change in thinking heralds a time to back off, to let our children unfold their new-found cerebral wings and take flight. They are well-equipped to leave the nest!

16

Volume 6

Lying
Volume 6, no. 1

Lying in childhood is a phase. However, if not handled correctly by adults, the phase could develop into a lifetime pattern. There are six basic rules for handling lying by children:

1. Don't try to force your child to tell the truth when you already know it.

2. Generally speaking, trying to force the child to tell the truth is a control battle the adult will lose.

3. Give your child more positive emotion for being honest than negative emotion for lying.

4. Consequence lying without anger.

5. Children may be consequenced for circumstantial evidence.

6. It is better to tell children we don't believe them than to tell them they are lying.

Let's start at the beginning. Many parents unconsciously make lying an issue by asking, "Is that the truth?" when there is really no solid reason to doubt the child. Sometimes when a child is dejected or down, parents might understandably say, "What's wrong?" The child, not wanting to talk, will say, "Oh, nothing."

At this point, it is not wise for the parent to say, "Is that the truth?" or "Don't you fib to me." The wise parent says instead, "Well, if you want to talk, I'm here."

Now let's look at the first rule: The most common mistake is trying to force the child to tell the truth when the parent already knows the truth. This almost always ends in a control battle that neither parent nor child feels good about. Often the child continues to lie, getting herself deeper and deeper into negative feelings with the parents.

See how the parent in the following exchange avoids a control battle centered around stolen cookies. This is done by assuming the child knows the parent knows the truth of the situation:

"Robert, come here. What did I tell you about these cookies?"

"Not to eat them, but I didn't."

"What did I tell you?"

"Not to eat them."

"Thank you! What did I say I was saving them for?"

"Paul's party."

"Right. This hacks me off. You hit your room right now and think things over."

"But . . ."

"Where do you need to go to think things over?"

"My room."

"Thank you! Bye."

The following is the same situation handled incorrectly:

"Robert, did you eat these cookies?"

"No!"

"Don't you lie to me!"

"I'm not!"

"Well, there are crumbs on the floor outside your room. How did they get there?"

"I don't know."

"You do too know. Why?"

"I don't know. I didn't do it!"

"Oh, yes you did. Now admit it! Robert, this kind of lying really makes me mad. You tell me the truth."

"I am."

"You are not! Did you eat these cookies?"

"(defiant) No!"

This goes on with the child becoming more resentful and the parent more frustrated. When a parent knows the truth, and try to get their child to admit it, it is a hidden way of saying, "I know you are going to continue to lie to me."

When a child has lied, restitution needs to be made. So if he has lied about taking something, it has to be given back with interest. If he has lied about taking a bath, he needs to go do it, and be late or miss school if necessary. (Parents—don't drive late kids!)

The consequence is handled coolly and as non-emotionally as possible so that when our children do tell the truth about a difficult issue we can say, "Wow, I bet that was hard to say! Thanks for the truth!" Our emotion is best reserved for when the child says or does something right.

Children can be "convicted" and consequenced on strong circumstantial evidence. Parents who find a candy wrapper in a child's room and allow the child to protest that he has not eaten any candy are almost asking for the child to lie. This is particularly true of the couple who said, "Well, we'll believe you this time, but not any more after this."

What kind of reasoning is that? If it was a lie the second time, why not the first? It would have been better for them to say, "We always take empty candy wrappers as evidence a person has eaten one. We think you need to give the whole thing some thought. If you still need to think about it at dinner time, no big deal."

Finally, it is better to tell a child, "I don't believe you," than to say, "You're lying." It's easy for a child to argue he is telling the truth, but he can't argue with the fact that you don't believe him.

Wise parents try to minimize the emotion centered around lying and avoid control battles they cannot win. If they know the child is lying, they express disappointment without anger and quietly consequence the child. They show positive emotion when the child tells the truth. They talk about themselves by saying, "I don't believe you," instead of talking about the child by saying, "You're lying."

The Six Rules for Handling Lying

1. Don't try to force your child to tell the truth when you already know it.

2. Generally speaking, trying to force the child—ever—to tell the truth is a control battle the adult will lose.

3. Give your child more positive emotion for being honest than negative emotion for lying.

4. Consequence lying without anger.

5. Children may be consequenced for circumstantial evidence.

6. It is better to tell children we don't believe them than to tell them they are lying.

Most adolescent back talk can be eliminated.
Foster shows you how as you read on.

Adolescent Back Talk
Volume 6, no. 2

Adolescents can be obnoxious, rebellious, and difficult! Some children back talk because we threaten their autonomy and independence. But if your child was basically good and loving before adolescence, or through fifth and sixth grade, then back talk almost certainly can be cleared up. This is done by listening to your child, and by giving your thoughts and ideas without trying to make her do it your way.

If we've had a good relationship with our children, deep down in their hearts they love and respect us and know we are usually right. If we give our adolescents both our love and the right to fail, most who have had a happy childhood will make mistakes and but will eventually choose success.

Our children will test us to see whether we will rescue them. But after finding out that we will continue lovingly to give our point of view, refuse to rescue, and in a non-angry way allow them to suffer the consequences of their behavior, most of the back talk will end.

One father recently said, "The more responsibility I give my son, without rescuing him, the nicer he acts. It's amazing!"

Talk with your children about the consequences of their decisions in a loving way. In the example you are about to read, the parent is trying to back off being overly-protective, while ensuring the child is responsible for his actions.

First, the parent has picked a moment when her child is in a relatively good mood. Perhaps she has taken the child out to breakfast, or they are alone together in the car.

Let's listen. Notice the mother is mainly asking questions, not giving a lecture. She starts by focusing on the child's feelings, not his back talk or tacky behavior. Our kids aren't willing to talk about their actions until they feel understood.

"Robert, sometimes you and I have a pretty hard time together. I'd really appreciate talking about that for a moment. What do you think the problem could be?"

"You're always on my case."

"Like how?"

"Like everything. You try to choose my friends and you tell me what to do all the time. EVERYTHING."

"Then how do you feel?"

"Like nothin' I do is right . . . "

"And then how to do act toward me?"

"I get mad, Mom."

"I know you do. I've been realizing, Robert, that I've always been trying to make sure you do the right thing and not get into any trouble. I've been trying to make sure you live a happy life. I realize I'm not giving you the right to blow it for yourself. I just wanted to apologize for that. Everyone has the right to make mistakes. I'm sòrry, Robert."

(stunned) "Well . . . that's OK, Mom."

"No, it isn't OK. It robs you of deciding for yourself when to come in or how important school is. And even if you dropped out of school, you'd probably get your adult degree before your were thirty. And if you were in detention or in trouble with the law, that wouldn't mean that I wouldn't get to visit you."

"Well, you should worry about some things. Like maybe I do drink too much at a few parties."

"I know. But that may not be a real big deal. Of course if I think you're drinking and driving, I'll just give your license plate number to the cops. No big deal. And if you have had too much to drink, don't come home until you're sober. I have trouble enough handling anyone around the house who has had too much to drink, so don't take it personally."

"Mom, get serious."

"I am serious. I love you too much to keep messing around trying to save you and make sure everything goes OK. Thanks for talking."

(a little doubtful) "Thanks . . . I guess."

In dealing with back talk, remember that all of us, including our children, have the inalienable right to protest. That is, we may not like paying taxes, and we may gripe, but we pay them. When parents accept their child's protest, the child often feels understood and does not need to up the ante to include direct disrespect. Let's listen:

"Paul, would you please empty the trash?"

"I hate emptying the trash. I do everything around here . . . It sucks!"

"I know, Honey. It's a bummer when there are always jobs to do. Thanks for doing it anyway."

This smart parent was thanking the child in advance. This technique works to eliminate smoking on airplanes and may work for your child. Society often thanks us for our cooperation before we actually give it!

Use of humor often defuses back talk or even disrespect. A wise teacher was once told by an angry student, "Screw yourself!" She thought for a moment—you could have heard a pin drop in the classroom—and then said, "I tried that years ago and it wasn't very gratifying." The child laughed and loved her thereafter. Sometimes when a child makes a common obscene comment, we can simply say, "Richard, you always have sex on your mind."

If a child's back talk and disrespect is extreme, it is sometimes best to simply let the child know that he may need to leave and come back when he can talk differently, that it is hard for the parent to take, and that it looks like the child is really having a hard time with the problem.

Notice how the wise parent says, "I have trouble listening to this," rather than, "Don't talk that way!" or "I won't have you talking like this!"

Now let's look at a different type of child. For some children, we need to respond to back talk in a different manner.

If a child's back talk is part of a number of other symptoms, including poor school behavior, use of drugs, or basic irresponsibility, then parental structure may need to be tightened and consequences may need to be imposed, not simply allowed to happen. In some cases, when children have severe problems, such as drug use or problems at school, professional help is needed.

If back talk starts in adolescence, it's almost always because we have not given the child enough opportunity to suffer from his own mistakes and learn from those mistakes. Adolescents who back talk generally have parents who get angry and then rescue them from the results of their mistakes.

In the next article, Foster presents how expectations formed in childhood play a major role in our parent/child relationships.

↵

Childhood Casts a Long Shadow into Adult Life
Volume 6, no. 3

Janice grew up in a home with a beautiful younger sister. The apple of her father's eye, the younger sister always seemed to rob Janice of her father's love. Donna's father abused and rejected her. Paul's father constantly traveled on business and never seemed to have time for him.

In their childhoods, each learned different lessons. Janice learned that younger, beautiful women steal the love we all deserve. Donna learned that men walk on women. Paul learned that fathers are absent and don't relate.

After they grew up, Janice, Donna, and Paul raised children with predictable problem behaviors. Arriving at my office, all wanted their kids fixed.

All three adults—bright folks themselves—recognized that parent/child interaction is important. But all concentrated mainly on their child's behavior, not on their own part of the interaction equation.

Janice was frustrated with her second child. Christie was a beautiful girl who was rebellious, negative, and angry toward her mother. Christie's manipulations and ability to charm her father drove a wedge between the husband and wife.

Donna's son, Tommy, was a difficult, angry child who drove his mother to distraction. Paul's son, Terry, was sullen and withdrawn.

In therapy, Janice saw that Christie robbed her of her husband's love exactly as her younger sister had robbed her of her father's love. However, she learned that she unconsciously expects this to happen, thinking, "Well, that makes sense. I'm always left out when important men in my life pay more attention to younger, more attractive females."

Donna saw that Tommy walked all over her just as her dad did. But she unconsciously expected this, thinking, "Well, that figures. All men are jerks."

Paul saw that his withdrawn son was distant, exactly as his own father had been. Paul accepted and expected this, thinking, "Well, fathers and sons often just aren't close."

Without an outside viewpoint, Janice would have lived a life of jealously and loneliness. Donna would have been walked on by men her whole life. And Paul would have forever yearned for father/son companionship.

Thus the specter of our own childhoods casts a long shadow into our adult lives. Our interaction patterns with both spouses and children are an outgrowth of childhood learning.

The process of enlightenment has predictable steps: First, we must get out of the habit of blaming others, and we must look at all the events in our lives as patterns. Second, we must see ourselves as weavers of the patterns.

Third, this realization must make us happy—because if we can weave one pattern, we can learn to weave another. We must take responsibility for the patterns in our lives.

Fourth, we must receive help from a good guide or companion. All of us, glowing with our own light, should understand that we can't see the shadows that we ourselves cast. The true picture can only be seen by another person who holds our hand, stands nearby, and looks at the situation from his or her own vantage point.

However, we can lovingly pay our parents back by casting our own light on their shadows!

In the next article, Foster tells you why the telephone is an excellent parenting tool.

Telephones
Volume 6, no. 4

Believe it or not, the telephone is a wonderful parenting instrument! Like all instruments, it can be appropriately used by parents to help children learn responsibility and to help them maintain a consistently cheerful demeanor. Or, it may inappropriately be used by parents and lead to numerous family hassels as well as a decrease in a child's self-image.

Early on, some children learn to associate the telephone with unhappiness. Other children learn to use the telephone to control their parents. In some unhappy families, the event that leads to rampant misbehavior is seeing Mom on the telephone.

Children sometimes think, "Now I can act up, out, and all around—she can't do anything about it because she's on the phone. And sure enough, Mom glares angrily at the child, covers the mouthpiece, and says in a frustrated voice, "Settle down!"

But the child knows that the phone is glued to Mom's earlobe. It's great! Mom's on her leash.

Because Mom has to continue talking and acting cheerfully, the child is free to cause minor furniture damage, pollute the auditory atmosphere, and generally behave in a way she never would get away with if Mom were not on the phone.

This control of parents often continues as the latency years slip into adolescence. Then the parent becomes frustrated because the child is on the phone "too much."

Parents are concerned because homework isn't getting done when the child talks too much on the phone. Parents worry that they can't get their calls because the child ties up the lines. Sometimes, affluent parents throw in the towel and pay the extra bucks to get their child a telephone in her own room.

From toddlerhood right through adolescence, children learn that when it comes to the phone, "Mom and Dad end up frustrated, and I end up winning." However, as Love and Logic principles dictate, there is no such thing as a win/lose situation between parent and child. There are only lose/lose or win/win situations.

Actually, the phone is an instrument that may be handled much differently. It can help the parents confirm to the child that they are in loving self-control. In turn, the child learn self-control and responsibility.

When a youngster starts acting up during a phone call, a wise parent says something along these lines: "I'm sorry, Joe. I'll need to phone you back. I have a situation here that I need to take care of. I'll be back with you in three minutes. Wait for my call. Thanks."

Then the parent puts the receiver down, walks over to the child and says with both eye contact and a firm voice, "Troy, I don't like the way you're acting when I'm on the phone. So, whip up to your room right now and stay there! I'll let you know when you can come out. You'll be there at least through this telephone call, and I'm hoping that it's a long one."

The point is that the child, early in life, learns that the parents have control of the phone, not that the phone controls the parents. This, of course, sets the stage for the parents to maintain control of phone issues during the child's adolescence.

With the low cost and availability of call-waiting, all parents with teens can now have an automatic, inexpensive, and efficient phone answering machine. As parents of adolescents know, their adolescent phone answering machine always circles around the phone. He is mega-available! Wise parents say to their teen:

> "Brent, you can use the phone as much as you want. Whenever any of us are on the line, we will answer the other line when it clicks and take a message for the other family member. (Since adolescents are on the phone for much longer periods than their parents, the kids, of course, end up being the home answering machine.)

"However, my dear child, there is a difference. When calls come in for you, I'll take the number and tell your friends that you'll call them back. But when a call comes in for an adult who is present in the home, you'll tell the caller that you're on the phone right now, but that you'll get off and immediately call the adult to the phone."

"Then, within two sentences, you'll tell your friend good-bye, tell him you'll call back, and immediately call the adult to take the phone call. Is the picture clear?"

"Yeah," responds the child. "It's clear, but it's unfair! How come you get to talk to people immediately and I have to wait?"

"That's because, my dear child, I pay the bills. Whoever pays the phone bill gets to use the phone immediately. It's their phone. If the rule seems unfair to you, you can pay for another line, pay the monthly bill or have your own phone in your room. (This is based on the supposition that any child responsible enough to earn his own money and pay for a separate line and monthly bill is responsible enough to have his own phone in his room. This is almost always true.)

Most children, considering the options, agree they should immediately call their parents to the phone. In return, they get to use the phone, which is a true privilege. Some teens, unfortunately, also need to have the following conversation with their parents:

"Stacy, if business associates or friends of mine call when you're home and on the phone, and they get either a busy signal or the phone just rings, what will we have to do to ensure that I always get my calls?"

"Well, I suppose you could ban me from the telephone so it would always ring through."

"What a good idea! Maybe we ought to give that some real thought. I appreciate the suggestion. Do you think we'll need that rule?"

"No, I guess not!"

"Thanks, Stacy. You're a jewel."

A loving parent/child relationship, firmness, and high expectations almost always ensure that you'll have a pleasant, courteous, and always-present answering machine if you have a teenager. Good luck!

17

Volume 7

Handling Anger
Volume 7, no. 1

I have been asked to give you ideas on how to handle your child's anger correctly. The correct response depends on three variables:

1. How old is your child?
2. What is the reason for the anger?
3. How is the anger being expressed?

Let's look at these issues one at a time

The first real anger parents need to be concerned with is the child's temper tantrums that begin at 9 months of age and which may continue until they climax at about 2-1/2 years old.

Before 9 months, if a child is angry, don't worry about it! Instead just fix the situation. The child needs to be dried out, washed off, or filled up.

At 9 months, however, the child first says by his actions, "I'm mad at you—no real good reason—and I'm going to yell my head off to prove it."

What don't we do? If we're wise, we don't tell the child to quit crying or quit being angry—that doesn't even work on my wife! Whenever we tell children what to do before they understand or will obey us, we are really simply saying, "Don't pay attention to me, my words are meaningless."

I once saw a mother and her 4-year-old sort of dragging each other across a parking lot. The kid was screaming and the mom, between the child's wails, would say, "Be quiet, Willie!" Any other 4-year-old watching would have said, "Hey, lady, he's not going to be quiet!"

In short, never tell a child what to do unless you definitely expect to be obeyed or can make the child obey!

We can tell a child where to go to have his fit—namely, away from us! That works well for my wife. She'll say, "Hey, Foster. I don't need this. I wish you'd take a hike." Awesome.

If it works for adults, it often works for kids. Parents, early in the child's life, may say, "John and Sarah, I really don't need this. I'd like you to whip up to your room, look in the mirror, and find an appreciative audience."

Of course, between 9 months and a year, we wouldn't say that. We'd just gently dump Bob in his bed and let him know that when he's been quiet 30 seconds or more, we'll be back to say, "Hi, guy, how're you doing?"

We are teaching the child that we don't like being around screaming people—that's just us! The child, then, grows up like us— expecting people not to scream at him either. Everyone ends up happy!

Letting a child know there's a limit to our tolerance of the expression of emotions should take place early in his life. Certainly before age two.

This brings us to the second issue. What is the reason for the child's anger? (Sometimes it's best to define it as "unhappiness.") If the child is unhappy about a situation and we can easily fix it by recognizing and accepting the emotions, let's do it. In these situations, we can say things like:

"I know it's a hassel for you to empty the trash. I understand—and thanks for doing it." (This illustrates a neat trick—recognizing the child's feelings while assuming compliance.)

"I know you're mad at me and I appreciate you letting me know. Now that I know that you know that I know how you feel, and I know that you know, I don't need to know more—so thanks for cooling off, pal. If you need to think about it more, whip up to your room and think about it there."

Finally, we have to ask ourselves, "How is this kid expressing her feelings, and is that acceptable? Remember, the United States government always gives us the right to moan and gripe. Others may leave because they don't like to hear it, but we do have the right.

Likewise, in parenting there's an important line between the assertive expression of anger—which we can encourage and even listen to while the other person vents—and the expression of disrespect, which we should discourage and not listen to a bit!

Even God discourages disrespect and taking His name in vain. If God doesn't like to handle it, we don't need to either. We can say, "Bill, I don't like hearing that kind of talk. It makes me feel a lot less like fixing you dinner. I think 'Gee, what am I doing, working over the stove for a person who feels that way about me?' It would spoil my own appetite to eat dinner with you. So I hope you'll join us for breakfast and figure out by then how you could have come across differently."

As parents, we walk the important line between being overly defensive and putting up with too much.

When our children's anger is directed to others, it's best to let the people involved work it out if it's at all possible. We try not to get involved in other people's problems or we become over-involved, co-dependent, or dysfunctional. And we all know that's tacky.

By the time a child reaches early adolescence, parents realize that a certain level of chronic, low-grade "snarkyness" is almost par for the course. Each of us has to figure out our own tolerance level.

At any rate, the following thought may be comforting or discomforting: For better or worse, the way we allow our children to express their feelings to us is the way they will express them to their first spouse.

The major rules for handling anger are: Never expect the child to handle anger better than you do yourselves; and don't tell the child to settle down—instead give choices and options, i.e., "If this . . . then this."

Listen when the child is content and respond. Let the child know there is no need to use anger to get your attention. Realize that adolescents often use an exclamation point when they really mean to use a question mark!

Foster's next article explains how to substitute consequences for "get backs."

ᴌᴐ

Parental Get-backs
Volume 7, no. 2

Parents tire of never-ending negative responses from their children. These responses range from toddlers biting others to older youngsters "forgetting" to do their chores.

Every so often I run into parents who want to "get back" at their little troop. This desire is usually carried out in an angry manner. I once knew of a frustrated mother who bit her four-year-old, screaming at the child, "There, how do you like it when someone bites you?"

Parents have been known to cuff an older child who has just hit a younger brother or sister. Parents of older children may, when the child refuses to do chores, angrily refuse to do something for the child: "Well, Buddy, you don't do your chores for me, so I'm not going to do such-and-such for you. So how does that feel to you?"

Such responses are born of parental frustration. While sometimes understandable, they are largely ineffective. Why is that? There are two reasons. First, children model adults. When adults use violence to cure violence, the child, modeling the adult, becomes more violent.

Second, parental anger reinforces the negative behavior. An angry parent is often a parent losing control. So who has the control? The child, of course. And giving a child such power, in itself, reinforces the negative behavior. Furthermore, such "get-backs" give the clear message, "I'll take care of you, Missy."

We don't want our children to take care of others! What we do want is to teach our children to take good care of themselves—to grow to be responsible and competent adults. However, effective get-backs can be carried out—under special circumstances:

The get-back must be carried out non-emotionally to take good care of the parents, not to prove something to the child.

Second, the get-back has to contain consequences that the child can choose to feel bad about. (When a child can choose to feel bad about a consequence, then he/she maintains constructive power.)

Finally, if the get-back involves "heavy" consequences, it should be used infrequently. If it doesn't work quickly, use a different technique or come at the issue from a different angle.

Lets's look at an example: Dan, age 11, does his chores sporadically. In fact, he told his mother he decided to skip some of them because they really weren't necessary. Dan's mother, after momentary anger, thoughtfully bit her tongue and answered, "What a thought! I probably have been doing things that really don't need doing, too. Good point."

Later in the week, Dan expected his mother to take him to a soccer game. Mom started to get her coat, then paused and said, "Oh, wait a minute. Sorry, Dan, I almost forgot. This is one of those things I decided really didn't need to be done."

Dan got the point. All chores were thereafter completed without hesitation. This was effective only because the mother took good care of herself, handled the situation matter-of-factly without anger, and allowed Dan to decide for himself if he was bothered by the consequence.

Roberta always forgets to pick up her clothes. "It's hard to remember to pick them up, Mom." Mom started picking them up for her. Roberta couldn't find them and asked Mom about them.

"Look, Honey. It's easy for you to forget to pick up that stuff. It's even harder for me to remember where I put them. I'm getting older, you know. My memory is even worse than yours."

"I probably either dropped them down the laundry chute, threw them in the corner of the back closet, or just stuffed them under your bed. Why don't you check them all—I know those clothes have to be somewhere! If they're not in any of those places, come back and tell me and I'll try to remember."

Although unorthodox and not highly recommended, Joyce's response to her 3-year-old was a thoughtful get-back that worked. Paula bit her mother. Hard. Joyce was about to become angry when she realized anger often makes the situation worse.

After three or four seconds of utter shock at her daughter's behavior, Joyce said, "Oh, Honey, I bet I taste like vanilla. Let me see what you taste like . . . "

Joyce bit Paula on the right arm. "Oh, yum, strawberry. You taste just great! What about your other arm . . . Oh yum, vanilla! Do you want to taste my other arm? No? Well, you can, you know. We can each enjoy tasting each other."

Paula never bit Joyce again. She decided for herself that those tasting parties just aren't that fun!

Consequences carried out in a matter-of-fact manner seldom lead to resentment in the child, and often result in changed behavior. Some consequences can be carried out with an almost joyful anticipation of the probable change in the child's future responses.

Not all daredevils are bad. In fact, one type is even desirable.
Foster explores daredevil behavior in the next article.

↵ꝛ

Raising Daredevil Kids
Volume 7, no. 3

No doubt the world is a dangerous place. Every day, the headlines tell us of more killings. In some cities, cars are being stolen even while people are in them.

It is understandable why most parents don't feel totally secure about the well-being of their children. Because there are more problems today, parents have become more watchful, careful, and protective. In fact, I have seen parents who are sometimes so vigilant in watching their children that simply "being vigilant" could be their full-time job!

It is also understandable that daredevil children raise vigilant parents. However, there is an easier way. Teach the child to be vigilant!

How do we do that? First, consider three types of children:

1. Children who would never be "daredevilish" and never take risks.

2. Death-defying little daredevils who are at high risk. (Death does not like to be defied very long!)

3. Daredevils who take thoughtful risks and have a slight chance of being hurt.

This last group of children might be compared to a daredevil who uses a safety net while on a flying trapeze. In other words, what they do looks pretty daring, but it is really pretty safe.

Children must be taught to be thoughtful daredevils, not death-defying daredevils, when they are 2 or 3. This is the stage of toddlerhood exploration. This is when parents start raising the three types of children listed above, and then, who, in turn, have their own buttons pushed by the child.

The first child, an individual who does not fully partake of life and never takes risks, is aided by a parent who is constantly worried. The parent's messages include:

"Be careful, you'll get hurt."

"Oh, John, you scared the wits out of me! Please don't do that!"

"The world is a scary place."

The second child—who may be at risk for death—is usually raised by a frightened parent who shows his worry with anger. When the child takes small risks in toddlerhood, the father angrily states:

"Stop that right now or you'll get a swat!"

"You make me so mad when you take those risks!"

All children, on an unconscious basis, like to make their parents angry. They really can't help themselves!

The third type of child, a little daredevil who takes thoughtful risks, is raised by a parent who states:

"If you do that, you might get hurt." (The parent then does not rescue.)

"John, honey, the way you are behaving, this could be goodbye. If you kill yourself, I'll miss you!"

In essence, the first parent's message tells the child, "The world is a scary place and I'm frightened for you."

The second parent, raising a rebellious and foolish child, says, "The world is a dangerous place and I'm mad at you!"

Finally, the third parent says, "The world may be a dangerous place, so I hope you watch out."

A word of caution as we watch our daredevil kids at play. Generally, we can sit back and make reasonable, thoughtful comments unless they are doing something that is likely to cause serious injury or death. Then immediate action is called for.

This is an issue that has to be carefully weighed, for the more severe the consequences, the more memorable the learning experience. But we don't want the child to remember it from heaven!

Avoiding control battles with our children
involves learning new skills. Foster presents these in the next article.

⌐⌐

Avoiding Control Battles
Volume 7, no. 4

Parents who have the happiest lives are the ones who best know how to avoid control battles.

Avoiding control battles is not always easy, but it is an essential, learnable skill. There are a few rules for avoiding control struggles:

1. Don't give an order that you cannot enforce.

2. Tell the child how you stand, rather than what she must do.

3. Give the child choices.

4. Problem-solve with your child while understanding your child's feelings.

5. Give only reasonable consequences that you can live with yourself.

6. If you've made a mistake with your child, admit it without overdoing the apology.

7. Avoid frustration and anger—a parent's expression of frustration and anger almost always means there has been a battle, and worse yet, the child has won!

Control battles often occur when parents give children orders they cannot make them follow. Such orders include: quit crying, pick up that stuff right now, move fast, etc.

No one can make a child or even an adult quit crying. Many children sigh and move slowly when asked to speed up. And kids tend to dawdle rather than doing it right now.

All these control battle statements would be avoided if the parents talked about themselves and where they stand, gave the child consequences, or gave the child choices.

Instead of orders, parents should start their sentences with the word "if" in most cases. "If" always can be used to indicate choices and consequences. For instance, the parent might say, "If you want to cry, whip up to your room," or "If you get your toys picked up by dinner, then you'll be eating with us," or "If you move really fast, I'll feel like moving fast for you and I'll start dinner."

Giving the child choices is an essential element in avoiding control battles. While giving choices, the wise parent talks about herself: "I like it when things are done quickly," or "I only like doing laundry that has been brought down to the laundry room," or "I always fix dinner for folks who have clean rooms."

Choices can be given for almost everything: "Would you like to wear your blue dress or your yellow dress to church?" "Would you like to hurry and leave with us or stay at home?"

Unwise parents set up control battles by saying things like, "We're leaving at 8:00; you've got to be ready!"

"Really. Don't bet on it," thinks every child in the world.

Even United Airlines doesn't say, "We're leaving at 8:00; you've got to be ready!" United says, "We're leaving at 8:00 and if you're there 10 minutes ahead of the departure, we won't give your seat away." Life is best filled with choices.

Control battles are avoided when parents and children problem-solve together. In the following example, the mother is problem-solving with the child about his belongings which are scattered throughout the room:

"Honey, do you have a minute?"

"Yeah, sure."

"Lately, you've been leaving your schoolwork scattered all through the house."

"Yeah, I know."

"What is a solution? What do you want to do about it?"

"Put it away, I guess."

"Well, that would be great! That would handle it this time. But this seems to be happening a lot. What do you want to do about it all the time?"

"Put it away after I leave it out."

"Well, that would be super. What if you still forget? It's easy to forget, you know."

"You pick it up?"

"Well, maybe I could. How about my just sort of sweeping through the place and putting all your stuff in a garbage bag and then putting it in the rec room? Then you'd know where it all is, and it would only take me a second."

(aghast) "All my books and shoes and stuff together?"

"Yeah, probably."

"I think I'll remember to pick it all up."

"Well, I hope so, but I do understand that forgetting is easy."

This mom avoided a control battle by problem-solving consequences without anger. It's simple once parents practice and get the knack.

It is extremely tacky to give consequences and then not be able to live with them. Parents sometimes tell their children they are going to send them to their room for the day and then call them out after an hour. Or, they ground children for two weeks and then relent after one week. These parents are covertly telling their children not to believe a word they say.

Control battles tend to be increased with parental anger, threats or expressions of frustration. They are decreased with choices, consequences, problem-solving and understanding of feelings.

18

Volume 8

Teaching "No"

Volume 8, no. 1

A young mother recently asked, "What do I do when my one-year-old stands up in the stroller?" She was wondering about using the word "no."

Simple as it might seem, the world of high achievement revolves around the learning of the concept of "no." Why?

- A successful life is built on self-discipline.

- Self-discipline is based on a person's ability to delay or deny self-gratification.

- Delay of self-gratification is built upon the individual's ability to say no to himself.

- The ability to say "no" to oneself is built upon the ability to accept "no" from early authority figures.

- The ability to accept "no" from authority in childhood is based upon the ability, during early toddlerhood, to obey and respect a parent's "no."

All in all, the learning of "no" is an essential cornerstone in the building of personality. Its importance cannot be overemphasized. Among the major problems now facing America is the vast number of young children who simply will not take "no" for an answer. They are obnoxious and disobedient to their parents in shopping centers and in shopping carts, in strollers and in living rooms across America.

These children who will not take "no" for an answer often grow into unproductive, irresponsible, self-indulgent individuals. They are unable to delay gratification and are often self-destructive to others as well as themselves.

There are several important rules for teaching "no":

- "No" should be learned before 13 months.

- It is fairly useless to try to teach "no" before 6 or 7 months of age.

- "No" must be stated correctly, at the right time, in the right way, for the right reasons.

Let's take a look at these rules one at a time. A child exceeds a dog in intelligence at about 9 months of age. At this time, a child is ready to learn no. This is the time of "Basic German Shepherd": Come, sit, go, no, stay.

Some parents attempt to teach "no" even before their child understands English! Then, as the child slowly begins to understand English in the last half of the first year, she has already learned that what comes out of the parents' mouth is meaningless nonsense!

This leads to the next rule of "no." "No" must be said only when the parent definitely expects the child to follow an order or can consequence the order in such a way that the order will be followed. Never, never say "no" unless you mean it and expect it to be followed. The consequence that leads the child to learn that the parent "means business" must be firm enough to ensure the correct behavior, but not more severe than necessary.

With all this information in mind, we are able to look at how to handle Henry when he stands up in his stroller and won't sit down. Does Henry need to be told "no"?

First, the intelligent parent decides whether the behavior is really unacceptable. The parent does not like Henry to stand in his stroller. He is jumping up and down on the seat like a nerd. However, the floor is carpeted. Mom may wisely decide to say, "Henry, I wish you wouldn't do that. You could have a big boom-boom."

Henry, hearing but not heeding, continues to jump up and down and gratifyingly falls on his noggin. He has a big boom-boom. He learns, "Oh, how wise my mother is." He also learns it's kind of stupid to jump up and down in a stroller. Who wants boom-booms?

However gratifying it is to allow children to suffer the natural consequences of their behavior, there are times that we, as parents, simply want the behavior to stop.

We must learn how to say "no" and mean it

Henry is jumping up and down on the seat of his stroller like a nerd. Cynthia, his mother, decides she does not have time to wait for the natural consequences, or that Henry simply has too good a sense of balance for a gratifying fall, or that the behavior is simply too obnoxious to put up with.

So, she says, without pleading and with firmness, "Henry, no." (Pleading parents always have disobedient and obnoxious children. The pleading, in and of itself, says, "I really don't expect to be obeyed.") At any rate, Henry, after looking briefly at Cynthia, grins at her foolishly and continues to jump, waiting (and secretly hoping) she will do something.

Cynthia does. She picks him up off the stroller, squeezing him uncomfortably, but not so uncomfortably that his juices run out, and puts him down, saying "I said 'no'."

If the trip to the floor was uncomfortable enough, Henry will not test and climb back up on the stroller and start jumping.

However, if Cynthia is queasy about "using force on a little kid just because I'm bigger than he is," or if Cynthia, from Henry's point of view, gratifyingly shouts, "I said 'no'!!!" to the point that Henry knows he has got her goat or pushed her button, then he'll scamper back up onto the stroller. At this point, he knows he is in control of his mother.

I feel strongly that it is at the age that a child stands in a stroller, or stands in a high chair, or gets into things shortly after he learns to walk, around the age of one, that an occasional pop on the rear may be in order. Professionals in my field are so afraid to give parents "permission" to correct through thoughtful and careful spanks that we've ended up with a generation of children who are abusive to their parents!

They are children who won't take "no" for an answer. Don't let it happen to you. Do it right. Do it when your children are about one year old. Mean business without being mean. Never say "no" unless you mean it.

Learn the keys to good Love and Logic parenting by reading on . . .

∽

Very Practical Advice on Raising Responsible Children
Volume 8, no. 2

Television, divorce, and two-career families have dramatically changed the requirements of effective parenting. Today, kids grow up more quickly and need to learn sooner how to cope with the challenges and pressures of contemporary society.

To help parents cope with these tremendous challenges, I'd like to answer the following questions:

What are the keys to good parenting in the 1990s?

There are two keys—love and logic. Children need love that is not permissive, that doesn't tolerate disrespect, and that is powerful enough to allow them to make mistakes and live with the consequences of those mistakes.

Logic has to do with the consequences of our children's actions. If we let our children live with the frustration, disappointment, and pain that logically follows their mistakes, they will learn from those mistakes.

Isn't that harsh?

Not if we support our children with compassionate empathy—not anger—as they learn these lessons. If young Danny misbehaves at the dinner table, he is offered the choice of eating nicely or playing on the floor. If he chooses the floor, he may become hungry later and his parents can be very sympathetic about it, promising a big breakfast the next day. Parenting with Love and Logic is a win-win philosophy.

What do you mean by win-win?

Parents win because they love in a healthy way and establish effective control over their kids without resorting to the anger and threats that bring on rebellious teen behavior. Kids win because they learn responsibility and the logic of life by solving their own problems. They acquire the tools for coping with the real world. In the process, parents and kids establish a rewarding relationship built on love and trust.

How can a toddler learn to be responsible?

Obviously, an infant is completely dependent, and parents must set limits only for safety's sake. However, toddlers can start making decisions about whether to get out of the tub now or a little later or whether to have plain or chocolate milk.

The limits we set should expand as our children grow older—they should receive more and more freedom and make more and more choices for themselves. If we have allowed them to learn from their earlier mistakes, they will make better choices as they grow up.

Can you give an example?

When a 6-year-old is dawdling with his food in the restaurant, holding up the family's shopping plans, angry words only give him a sense of power over his parents. A Love and Logic parent would give him a realistic choice. The father might say (with a smile), "Son, I'm leaving in five minutes. You can come with me hungry or come with me full. You decide." The parents will not nag after that.

When it's time to go, the father offers another set of choices: "Leave with me under your own power or under my power." And, if necessary, the father simply picks the boy up and carries him out. No angry words are spoken. If the boy later complains of hunger, the parents are very sympathetic, but don't give him anything to eat. They might commiserate with him, admitting they too get hungry after missing a meal.

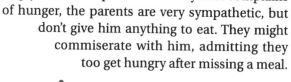

What if, as a parent, you don't like one of the choices?

There is an art to offering choices. First and foremost, always select choices you can live with. Follow these general guidelines:

Never offer a choice you aren't willing to let the child experience the consequences of.

Never offer choices when the child is in danger.

Be aware that there is always a third choice—you will make the choice if the child won't.

Don't offer choices in anger. Use phrases such as, "You're welcome to rake the lawn so I'll have time to clean your room," "Feel free to go to the playground as soon as you have walked the dog," or "What would be best for you—to spend your allowance on fun this week or pay someone to do your chores?"

This sounds great here—but don't children provoke their parents into using this method too often?

It takes practice to be a Love and Logic parent. Anger, however, only teaches children that messing up makes adults mad. And, it makes their problems our problems, which tells them they are not capable of coping.

Try to distinguish between fighting words ("No, you can't go out to play until your chores are done"), and thinking words ("Yes, you may go out to play as soon as your chores are done").

Practice sympathizing with your child's plight rather than being angry. When your son gets low grades on his report card, the angry response would be to say that he'll have to stay in every afternoon and do his lessons under your supervision. You are really telling him that he can't do the work without your help and discipline.

A better, more enthusiastic response would be, "Oh, how awful. You must feel terrible. What can you do?" This way, you are letting the child, with your sympathetic support, solve his own problem. He will gain self-respect as well as better work habits and better grades.

What if your children are already teenagers when you start experimenting with Love and Logic parenting?

It's never too late to use Love and Logic. It will take more thinking and patience, but you will grow as much as your children do in the process. And, you will be building a loving and respectful relationship that will last far beyond the teen years.

(Reprinted with the permission of Bottom Line/Personal, 330 W. 42nd St., New York, N.Y. 10036)

A child's separation problems are among the most difficult for parents to handle. Foster discusses separation in the next article.

∽

Your Child's Problems with Separation
Volume 8, no. 3

This article concerns your child's problems with separation. This topic is important, for there are few situations as difficult for parents to face as a whiny, clingy, terrified child who is frightened to stay with strangers, go to bed, or head off to preschool.

Not only is this situation distressing, it is universal. Almost all parents have to deal with this problem at some time, since almost all children go through periods of separation anxiety. Such anxiety may occur under a number of different names, and the parent might not even realize the basic issue is fear of separation.

Thus, school phobias, fear of going to bed, fear of new places/situations, and fear of being left alone may all be separation problems masquerading under different names.

There are four main reasons for separation problems:

1. First, separation anxiety at certain stages in life may be normal. For instance, it is absolutely normal in a 7- or 8-month-old infant and, in fact, may be taken as a sign that normal mother/child bonding is taking place.

Conversely, when small children happily walk off with any stranger, it may be a sign of attachment or bonding difficulties. Separation anxiety at 7 or 8 months is generally known as "stranger anxiety." It takes place when a child can recognize that a person other than his mom is taking him away from the person who has always provided food and love.

2. Some children may be genetically predisposed to experience more separation anxiety than others. Although, to my knowledge, this has not been studied, it is known that genetics play a strong role in many personality traits. Intelligence, aggressiveness, and shyness, for example, all have genetic roots.

3. There are environmental circumstances that may play a role in separation anxiety. Small children often have more separation problems after their parents' divorce or after a parent has taken a job and is more frequently away from home. Such anxiety might be considered "normal regression."

Sometimes children have separation anxiety for a good reason: The person they have been left with is abusive. Thus, children may be afraid to go off to preschool, to be left with the mother's boyfriend, etc. Child abuse appears to be more rampant now than at any time in the past.

4. Finally, we come to the fourth reason for separation anxiety: parental response. Parental response may not only be responsible for the onset of separation anxiety, but even more frequently it may turn a simple time-limited "stage" into a lifetime pattern of fearfulness.

In my experience, separation anxiety has more to do with parental response than the other three issues combined. I often tell parents I hope the child's problem is the result of parental response because this is something they can change!

However, if separation anxiety is a response to a difficult environment or is something intrinsic to the child's personality, it is much more difficult to turn the problem around.

Since most parents do their best to help their children cope with separation anxiety, how is it that the parental response so frequently makes the problem worse?

First, children live on parental emotions. Whatever behavior causes parental emotion is more frequently displayed. And nothing causes more parental emotion than a terrified child. Parents themselves become distraught and terrified of the child's terror.

Sometimes parents mistakenly believe that it is only their own happiness and joy that can increase a child's behavior. They believe that if they are distraught or angry they will decrease the behavior that brought about the parental response. This is absolutely wrong. Any parental emotion reinforces a particular childhood behavior.

A young father named Roger questioned me about the problems he was having with his three-year-old daughter who was having trouble going to bed. Roger had tried everything—from reading her stories, pleading with her, staying with her in his room, and angrily demanding that she go to bed.

All his efforts were to no avail. The problem was getting worse. I told Roger to simply sit down with his daughter and ask her why she was afraid, and matter-of-factly talk the situation over with her. At the end of his discussion with her and exploration of her fears, he was to tell her—again matter-of-factly and firmly—that he expected her to go to bed and stay there.

The next day Roger came to me glowing with happiness. "It was so easy! It worked so well. I can't believe how this child was feeding off my emotions. I was both angry and distraught. I made the situation worse and never realized it. Boy, this idea of exploring the child's feelings and then expecting them to cope with them works like magic."

Second, children buy into their parent's unconscious belief systems. Many parents validate a child's separation anxiety by unconsciously buying into the "reasonableness of it all." This is often carried out by communicating over-reassurance to the child.

Whenever I see children in the office, I walk up to them and say, "Hi, I'm Dr. Cline." I shake the child's hand, turn, and start to walk to my office with the assumption that the child is following me.

This is always true unless I hear a soft voice, generally the mother's, saying, "It'll be OK." Whenever I hear the mother say that, I know the child will remain glued to the waiting room chair. The hidden assumption behind the mother's assurance is that the child needs reassurance. And the hidden assumption behind needing reassurance is that there is something very real and frightening out there.

Third, through separation anxiety, children act out hidden or vaguely recognized parental fears.

Julie moved to a small town after living in the city. She felt shoved into the move because of her husband's career change. In the new town, she had no friends and felt lonely. Guess what? Julie's little boy, David, had fears about going to school. Why? He didn't know anybody and wouldn't have any friends.

Julie could not handle David's separation anxiety because he was acting out her own belief system. Unconsciously, a parent has a very difficult time dealing with her child's fear when the child has "every right" to that fear. This includes all kinds of strange fears that children ordinarily should never have: fear of nuclear war, fear of the increased number of abortions, fear of divorce, even fear of a stock market crash.

Once a child hones in on a parental fear, most parents are at a complete loss and may attempt, very unconvincingly, to reassure the child while validating the fear every minute of the interaction!

Often parents become distraught and ineffective when a child manifests a fear they themselves had in their own childhood. One mother said, "I don't think his fears are foolish at all. I think they're very real." This mother didn't think the fears were foolish because they were similar to fears she had experienced in her own childhood.

However, the fears were extremely foolish and, at the same time, very real. Much separation anxiety is foolish but real. Many parents believe it either has to be sensible and real, or irrational and unreal. Instead, the fear should be treated as irrational and very real for the child.

Jeannette had a son named Todd who was extremely fearful of going to school. Jeannette handled this with reassurance and motherly concern. The problem got worse. After attending a Love and Logic parenting class, she took a new approach and said, "Well, Todd, I'm sure these are very real fears for you, and I hope you can cope with them. I'm sure glad I don't have fears like that! Good luck."

At first, Todd was very upset his mother couldn't be more sympathetic. But it took him only a week to overcome his fears.

Wise parents realize their children pick up on their own belief systems and that parental emotion feeds almost any childhood behavior. Finally, wise parents know they must clearly separate out who has the problem—parent or child.

To spank or not to spank? Read Foster's advice in the next article.

Thoughts on Popping a Kid
Volume 8, no. 4

I am constantly amazed by the number of therapists who raise children that most thinking beings would rather not take off the shelf. Why is this?

The other day I saw a social worker with a little beast that only a mother could love. The child was running around completely out of control while the mom stood by with a hopeless and helpless "what's a mother to do?" look on her face. I wondered out loud to her if she had ever given him a whop on the rear. She gave me that aghast and horrified look only therapists can give when the issue of spanking is raised.

Then she announced, in the immediate reframing that almost always takes place on this issue, "I don't believe in beating children."

"Well, hey, Cynthia, who does?"

The only thing I can figure out is that therapists so often deal with abusive parents that they have lost their perspective on this issue. Spanking has even become a forbidden subject for therapists to write about. I am taking my professional life in my hands by penning this simple article!

I believe the way the thinking goes is this: "Abusive parents beat their children; abuse often involves striking a child; giving a child a pop is one way of striking a child. Therefore, anyone who gives a child a pop is abusive." This type of reasoning, like so much I see these days, would not receive enthusiastic approval in a class on logic.

Sweden, as you may know, outlawed ever popping children. Social workers can more easily remove a child from the home there than can social workers in America. So with this wonderful law, they must have a wonderful world of outstanding citizens over there. Right? Wrong!

There are many aspects of Sweden's society that are breaking down. Non-marital unions are up markedly, with a huge increase in non-marital cohabitation among childbearing couples. Sweden has one of the highest percentages of children born out of wedlock in the industrial world—over 50 percent, compared with 22 percent in the United States.

Parental authority has shifted heavily to the state. Sweden probably has the world's lowest percentage of households with extended families. Swedish delinquency rates are up abruptly, along with related youth depression, suicide, and alcoholism. (David Popenoe, *The Public Interest,* Vol. 102, Winter 1991.)

I want to state clearly for the record that popping a child on the rear, in and of itself, is definitely not child abuse! However, it does have major disadvantages:

Because it is a strong technique, there may nothing left to use next. You have used up your last "big gun."

Spanking may lead to resentment instead of learning.

Spanking is less effective or not effective at all with frequent or continued use.

Spanking may mean that the child is in control, not the parent.

So why ever do it?

In thinking about this issue, I have come to believe, frankly, that it is not the use of spanking that is helpful. It is more likely the fact that it could be used. This is a fine, but very important distinction. Also, how are we to know if something may be useful unless it is tried at least once?

During my 20 years in practice, I have found that the really great parents don't go around spanking their kids. But all of them have popped their kids once or so. None of these great parents are horrified at the idea of spanking; they just don't feel the need to do it. It is, in essence, no big deal. But given the proper situation, they would be willing to do it. And their kids know it!

I often think about the last 10 years, and recognize them, as we all do, as the first time in history that the major powers did not engage in war. Meanwhile, the little nations have continued to kill each other off at the usual rate.

The major nations both had nuclear weapons. Both knew the other was willing to use those awful things. And yet there was no war. Nuclear weapons were only used twice. No doubt they will be misused, in one way or another, in the future. But that doesn't negate my main point. Force is effective if it can be used, but it does not always need to be carried out.

The only reason I am writing this little note to you dear readers is because I believe it is my profession that has led good, non-abusive parents to believe it is their lot in life to raise bratty kids. My dear 30-year-old daughter told me the following story:

> I was playing in the park with Kathryn. Over on the merry-go-round sat another young mother with her small child on her lap. From a short distance, I watched this mother being hassled by her little girl, who was both fidgety and obnoxious, and who reached up now and then to strike at her mother's face.

> The mother attempted to talk and plead with the little toddler, which of course went no place. At long last, to my way of thinking, the mom finally turned the kid over and gave her a whop on the fanny. The child cried, the mother held her and whispered sweet nothings in her little ear, and soon all was sunny.

Shortly thereafter, the mother and I were swinging our little girls next to each other and talking. The other young mom said a little apologetically that she guessed I had seen her little to-do with her daughter. I laughed and said, "Yes."

The mom said her little girl was infrequently obnoxious. I asked her if should would like my thoughts. She smiled and said, "Yes." I told her that she had done the right thing—she had just waited too long to do it! She looked relieved and then said, "Oh, I know. I wanted to do it sooner, but I was afraid you would think I was an abusive mother."

Enough said!

19

Volume 9

Understanding Underachievers
Volume 9, no. 1

Generally, when we think of underachievement, we think of school under-achievement. However, many children underachieve at home. That is, they just don't do things right at home—whether it be finishing their chores or remembering to pick up after themselves.

At home, like school, there may be a problem getting the job done right. Some children actually do quite well washing the dishes, cleaning off the table, and accomplishing their other chores. Thus, in understanding school underachievement the two great categories are 1) children who underachieve both at home and at school, and 2) children who underachieve primarily at school.

If a child is underachieving in all environments, forget about school. Such a child needs to be understood. Does he have trouble figuring things out in general? Does he have a poor attitude? Is there some of both? Is there a problem in his parenting or problems in his early history?

In essence, when a child underachieves across the board it is important to look at both the child and the parent/child relationship. It is not necessary to focus on the school.

When children underachieve primarily at school, they must be divided into two large groups: 1) those with poor attitudes and 2) those with good attitudes.

The children with poor attitudes need to be further divided into three groups: 1) those who have a poor attitude toward all subjects; 2) those who have a poor attitude toward certain subjects; and 3) those who have a poor attitude toward teachers.

If a child has a poor attitude toward all subjects, then her attitude needs to be examined. Sometimes children who have a learning disorder have poor attitudes. Certainly, most adults who have problems at a particular task and find themselves continually being compared to others who do the task better develop poor attitudes.

There is a possibility that a child with both a good attitude in school and a poor attitude toward subjects or teachers has a learning disorder. Children who have trouble learning are divided into those who have normal IQs and those who have low IQs.

Sometimes a child with a low IQ is very spotty. That is, she has some areas that are above average and some areas that are below average. In general, children who have low IQs because they are extremely "spotty" on IQ tests have a better prognosis, in the long run, than children who have low IQs because they are low "across the board." After all, if a child is good in some areas, as an adult she may rely on those areas of strengths.

Next, it is important to examine a child's handwriting. Children with poor handwriting are divided into two groups: 1) those who are impulsive, fragmented and have trouble focusing, and 2) children who are not impulsive and have no trouble focusing.

If a child has poor handwriting and is impulsive (such children often have a poor attitude about school in general), Attention Deficit Disorder with or without hyperactivity should be considered. This is more common in boys than in girls. When Attention Deficit Disorder is present in girls, they are less likely to be hyperactive.

Children with poor handwriting should have their ability to copy figures examined. Generally speaking, children can draw circles at 3, squares at 4, triangles at 5 and diamonds at 6. If a child has trouble copying geometric figures, the child should be examined by a professional for a possible learning disorder.

If your child does have a learning disorder, it is important to know whether she is suffering from a learning lag or a learning deficit. Children suffering from learning lags often learn to walk relatively late and may have a history of late talking and poor sentence construction. The child's learning problem is more likely to be a lag if all of these early problems have "caught up."

On the other hand, if the child has had early problems and they have not caught up, or if she has a low IQ in general, then a learning deficit is more likely to be present.

Luckily, on all these issues, parents are able to benefit from wise counseling. Sometimes the emphasis must be placed on helping the child accept the problems and work around them. Less often, remediation may help. In any event, the problem is more easily handled when both parents and children know what to expect and what the future probably holds.

Love, affection, and food should go hand-in-hand. In his next article, Foster shares his wisdom on how to avoid conflicts around food

✍

Finish Your Beets, I Only Gave You a Little Bit!
Volume 9, no. 2

As your basic child psychiatrist, I feel sadder about family disagreements surrounding food than any other single issue. Such fights are generally unnecessary and so easily prevented.

Furthermore, the sharing of food and love is universal. When people fight about food, the connection between love and food is lost. I will give you four guidelines on handling food, but first I want to explore some important, general thoughts about food.

There are many examples of the connection between food and love. We say, "I love you, Sweetheart," or "I love you, Honey. You're the frosting on my cake."

When we want to be friends with someone, we say, "Let's go out for a drink," or "Let's go to dinner together." Naming a child Candy may be carrying these oral aspects of love about as far as they can go.

The point is, love, affection, and food should go hand-in-hand. John Stewart Mills, Jack Kennedy, and many others discuss the importance of dinnertime conversation in their later writing. Too many of us eat in a rush. In the old days, families would sit and talk, recapping the day, spinning yarns, enjoying each other.

Guideline 1

SAYING, "TRY IT, YOU'LL LIKE IT," IS UNHELPFUL AND GENERALLY NOT TRUE

People's tastes naturally change with age, not through learning. Children and adults have taste buds of different sensitivity. One doesn't find the average child lapping up eggplant, some cheeses or sweetbreads. About one-fourth of all adults remember, as kids, not being able to stomach the feel of tapioca in their mouths. To some kids it simply feels "gushy, icky."

As a child, I remember my grandfather telling me to put a pill "way back in the back of your mouth so you won't taste it—back there by the back of your tongue." So I tried it. Was I ever surprised! I thought, "My grandpa lied!" He thought I wouldn't taste it.

Children's and adults' taste buds not only differ in sensitivity, but also in placement. Kids often look like chipmunks with gumballs rammed back into the angle of their jaw because that's where they taste food. You don't see that in the average nursing home. As we grow older, we taste most acutely on the tips of our tongues.

Guideline 2

GIVE INFORMATION ABOUT FOOD BEFORE PROHIBITIONS AND ORDERS

For instance, it might be wise to say, "When kids eat so little before dessert and then eat a lot of dessert, they don't get much vitamin D. Their bones turn soft—I mean you could probably still walk, Jake, without collapsing on yourself, but I'm sure glad I eat good stuff before I layer it with sugar or I might be pretty weak myself!"

With the little sugarholic, we may have to use some rules. But as wise parents, we avoid using rules whenever possible. We realize that as our children grow older, we will never, but never, be able to control what they put into their mouths. Kids must learn to make their own good rules.

Guideline 3

ANGER AND FRUSTRATION AROUND FOOD ISSUES ALMOST ALWAYS MAKE THE PROBLEM WORSE

I'll never forget a mother who brought her child to see me. While I talked to her, the son waited outside the room, evidently buying a soda. When his mother finished her part of the session, she left my office and spied him sipping his soda, quietly reading a magazine.

The mom practically became hysterical. "He'll become hyper, he'll become hyper," she wailed. Right then her son started visibly shaking. I was shaking. The mother was shaking. We were all hyper.

In contrast, I remember a parent saying, "Wow! You didn't eat any sweets until dinnertime! I bet you're proud of yourself! That's hard!"

Guideline 4

USE NATURAL CONSEQUENCES FOR FOOD FADS/FOOD PROBLEMS ONLY IF ENCOURAGEMENT AND TALKING THINGS OVER HAS NOT WORKED

Parents can use consequences, if necessary, mainly to take care of themselves. Consider the following:

> "If all you want to eat is hamburger, you'll probably need to fix it yourself."

> "I'll pay for one-half of all the sugar-coated flakes you want. If you want them bad enough to earn the other half of what they cost, great!"

> "I don't like fixing meals for people who aren't hungry because they've gorged on sweets before their meal. So how would you feel if I fixed my meal and you fixed yours for a while?"

Most of us eat what we need. Obesity and weight problems often correlate with genetics. Keeping this in mind, we realize that many food fights with our children are avoidable and unnecessary.

> *How much do parents have to put up with?*
> *Foster explores this question in the next article.*

سمی

Freedom of Speech and Disrespect
Volume 9, no. 3

What kind of childhood behavior does everyone want and expect? That question used to be easy to answer. In the past, parents wanted and expected children who were nice (to the parents), sweet (for the parents), and, in general, even polite.

These expectations were carried to such an extreme that most parents expected children to be seen and not heard. Overall, parents expected kids who didn't whine or argue and who quickly and quietly did as they were asked.

However, in more modern times, parents have been told to lower their expectations, and that it is of primary importance to meet their children's needs. Not just some of them—if you are a good parent—all of them! And so the need came to be defined by the child rather than the adult.

This causes real problems because many adults don't know the difference between a child's wants and needs. This has happened all across America as individuals have redefined their wants and pursuits as basic rights and needs. In the world of modern psychology, some authorities even intimate that if children seem responsive, motivated, cheerful and quickly obedient, they must have something wrong with them deep down inside, or they are overly inhibited or have some psychological problem.

In short, modern parents are constantly bombarded with articles that insist they be ever mindful of "what's good for the child." Complicating this is the fact that as the level of expected responsibility and self-discipline has been lowered for all citizens, it almost goes against the grain of American culture even to suggest that children should be self-disciplined, responsible, well-behaved, mindful, and responsive to adults.

One parent recently asked, "Are there kids like that, or is it all wishful thinking?" What was taken as common and expected behavior on the farm, where kids contributed to the operation, is now so rare it would be considered either a myth or a sign of psychopathology.

After a recent speaking engagement in which I had mentioned the importance of well-disciplined children, an angry father came up to me ranting and raving that Love and Logic methods, "don't give the child the right to protest." However, this guy was not simply protesting, he was being downright rude and obnoxious. I'll bet that when his own kids are rude and obnoxious, he confuses it with protest.

Love and Logic methods emphasize the importance of children developing respect and obedience. However, children always have the right to protest. It is easy, though, for some parents to confuse the child's right to protest with the right to be whiny, negative, and obnoxious.

And there are other issues that many be confused. This confusion occurs when adults use rationalizations and redefinitions to validate a wide variety of obnoxious, disrespectful, and disobedient childhood behavior.

When a child became pouty following a reprimand, one mother redefined his behavior as "sensitive." But being sensitive isn't about going around with a long face. Being sensitive means caring about another person's misery. I often see these "sensitive" kids making other people miserable.

One father, after enduring his son's disrespect in silence, turned and said with a perhaps a little embarrassment, "Boys will be boys." I said, "Hey, Ralph, that's sexist! And why should boys be turkeys?"

After one of my talks, a mother asked a question about her two girls who constantly put each other down. "They're very competitive," noted the mother. Children being nasty to each other, however, is not a sign of being competitive. To say it is competitive behavior, rather than simply calling it unacceptable behavior, again covertly encourages the nasty behavior. Bruce Jenner, one of the greatest competitors of all time, never went around putting people down!

Finally, when children are testing the limits and are in need of discipline, I have heard more than one parent put up with the behavior and covertly OK it by saying: "I don't want to break her spirit." I remember thinking that the other adults who were nearby were probably saying to themselves, "Gee, Jenny, we wouldn't want you to break her spirit either. We would just like you to bottle and cork it for a bit!"

Sometimes parents feel bound to put up with nonsense because they feel their child has a right to "freedom of speech." Actually, in a family context, freedom of speech is irrelevant. It is only relevant in a political context.

Politically, in America, freedom of speech allows people to be downright rude and obnoxious. Citizens can exercise their freedom of speech by burning flags and bras. Our freedom of speech laws ensure that citizens won't get locked up for these activities—but who among us would want to take these folks home and live with them? While it may be politically acceptable to burn a flag or bra at a rally, it may be most unacceptable to do it in the living room!

And this is true with much obnoxious and rude behavior. A flag burner can do it outside. Likewise, when a kid is rude and obnoxious, the parent has the right to say, "Hey, Jake, take it outside!" In a public situation, when citizens express their freedom of speech in an obnoxious way, the rest of the population has the right to walk away. But a home gets a little cramped, and whoever owns the home has the ultimate right to ask the other person to walk away.

There are a number of reasons why parents confuse lack of respect with freedom of speech; pouting with sensitivity; nasty sibling behavior with competition; and marginally unacceptable behavior with "demonstrating spirit." Many of these reasons are unconscious. This will be the subject of our next article.

Understanding Why Parents Put Up With Nonsense
Volume 9, no. 4

"Why does that parent put up with that?" we sometimes find ourselves wondering as we watch parents and their children interact.

In the last issue, I discussed the surface rationalizations that parents sometimes use to excuse their children's obnoxious behavior. However, there are deeper reasons, many of them unconscious, that lead some parents to put up with a lot more than they should from their children.

The unconscious need to be needed

Some adults, especially those from dysfunctional or neglectful homes, are not sure that anyone really wants to be around them. Those who felt neglected or rejected as children tend to be ultra-sensitive to these feelings as adults. They do everything possible to avoid feeling left out, neglected, or rejected.

Unconsciously, the best way we make sure we're not left out is to make sure someone needs us. There is a song that says, "People who need people are the luckiest people in the world." But don't bet on it! There are many problem people who lock into the "need to be needed" and develop co-dependent and symbiotic relationships.

It is probably a lot healthier to want to be wanted. Parents who need to be needed may consciously infantilize their children: "Roger is so lucky I am here to look out for him!" Rather than encouraging mature, self-reliant behavior, such parents tend to promote immature and dependent behavior.

When Eleanor was growing up, she was frequently left to fend for herself by a self-centered and distant mother. As a lonely little girl, she made the decision that her own child would always feel loved and cared for. To avoid her parents' mistakes, Eleanor swung the pendulum far in the opposite direction by giving her daughter too much attention. The result was a child who was demanding, obnoxious, and non-compliant.

While trying to meet her daughter's increasing demands for attention and avoid her mother's mistakes, Eleanor had raised a self-centered little girl who would go on to neglect her own daughter. As is so often the case, where the pendulum is swung between the generations, the child raises the spitting image of her own parents.

What's "normal"?

All parents have different ideas of what goes on in a "normal" home. The norm we generally accept or reject is formed largely in our own childhood. Some parents attempt to justify a child's angry and disrespectful behavior by noting, "It's only normal." Sometimes angry adolescent behavior is accepted by a parent who muses, "I don't like it, but I guess it's normal—I remember what I was like as a kid."

Although Beaver Cleaver's family, the Brady Bunch, and the Cosbys are now considered hopelessly outdated, they nevertheless represent the values that many of us grew up with. Such functional families may no longer be the norm, but at one time they were!

In reality, folks don't decide what's normal by watching TV, but rather from the way they were raised. You can bet that those professionals who most loudly criticize the Cleaver family image never grew up around such love themselves.

Parental self-image

Parental self-image plays a large role in what we will accept and expect from our children. When folks grow up being treated as if they are important and deserve respect, they tend to naturally expect the same from those around them throughout life.

Thus, when Junior is loud and demanding most people think to themselves: "When I was a kid, I wasn't treated poorly, and I sure don't expect or accept it from you, either, Kiddo."

When parents were mistreated, yelled at, ignored, or discounted as children, they often have a strong tendency to be angry at and overly sensitive to disrespect from the children, while unconsciously accepting the children's behavior as justified.

Such parents continually ask themselves, "What am I doing wrong?" Thus, the woman who had an obnoxious and controlling father is at risk for raising an obnoxious and controlling son. When the child complains and whines, such parents try harder, instead of saying, "Boy, Roger, you appear to be doing lots of things wrong. I hope you'll try harder!"

Parental guilt

I recently talked with Susan, who asked me how she should handle her out-of-control daughter. Susan herself was a fairly pleasant, low-key, and accepting lady who really didn't "deserve" her child's downright disrespect. The more I talked with her, I realized she had great difficulty in setting limits, saying "no" and meaning business.

As we looked at the issues in more depth, it became clear that Susan was guilt-ridden over her divorce. "When I look at my daughter's behavior, I realize it is the result of my divorce," she said.

Once parents think they have "caused" the problem, they have a great deal of difficulty coping with it. They think, "If it weren't for me, he wouldn't be acting this way in the first place, so how can I give him any consequences?"

I have seen working parents accept hideous acting out, "because I know I should be giving him more of my attention." Granted, some children may need and even "deserve" more quality time, but excusing miserable behavior because "Mom isn't home more" simply compounds the problem.

When parents feel guilty, they often feel incapacitated and can't bring themselves to be effective. This is especially true when corrective consequences might lead their child to feel temporarily unhappy.

When basically good people become parents and chronically accept disrespect from the children, it is almost always driven by unconscious needs, expectations, and issues present in the parent's own childhood.

20

Volume 10

Changing My Mind About the Dangers of Kids and TV
Volume 10, no. 1

I'm beginning to change my mind about whether TV is dangerous to American children.

During the last 20 years of practice, I have viewed all the ruckus about children and TV violence as pretty alarmist and somewhat silly. Over the years, I told parents that I had seen a lot more psychic blood spilled around the boob tube, as parents and children fight about what can or cannot be watched, than I had in the programs themselves.

Further, as far as I know, there is not one really good controlled study that shows that violence on TV begets violence in normal children. As heaven knows, there has been a bevy of researchers who have been trying to prove that hypothesis.

In 20 years of practicing therapy at Evergreen Consultants, I have never seen even one child whose violence was caused by TV. (Naturally, violent children get off on violent TV. But then, they also get off on bashing other kids, too. Let's not confuse cause and effect. Such children display just as great a propensity for violence when they are placed in one of our trained foster homes where there is no TV.)

The violence of a football game is worse than the violence of the cartoons that some parents get all lathered up about. Some therapists even ask children to act out their most violent fantasies in play therapy as an emotional outlet.

Likewise, I've never had even one patient say to me, "You know, Foster, I grew up in a really dysfunctional family, but I watched Cosby, Beaver Cleaver, and the Brady Bunch. That's why I turned out so great!"

I always gave my own (now grown) birth children the "can do" message. That is, when they watched stuff I really didn't approve of, I just let them know that if anyone could handle the sex and violence on TV, they could. Their brains would never turn to butter, their genes were just too good.

I let them know that no matter what went on with their peers or on TV, they would turn out great! And they have! All are strong Christian adults, saying to their own kids, "You want to watch that stuff? I'm glad I don't!" Then they leave the choice and the consequences up to their children.

Intention—not attention—disorder

But I am starting to change my mind about the dangers of TV. I don't think it's a matter of *what* children watch on TV, but *that they watch so much*. I think that when children are ages 3 to 6, spending hours in front of the TV may be wrecking their brains. It doesn't matter whether the show is a "bad" one or a "good" Disney program. I think it is the *process of watching* that is harmful.

Attention Deficit Disorder (ADD) in children has presently become a national epidemic. ADD is a fairly serious problem and may be related to an old diagnosis of minimal brain damage.

After seeing hundreds of these children at Evergreen Consultants, we are starting to realize that many do not really have an attention deficit disorder. Rather, they have an intention disorder. That is, the problem appears when the children are required to perform a task or to complete a job.

Attention itself may actually be quite unimpaired. Such a child can play Nintendo, no problem; watch a TV program, no problem; even pay attention to a teacher, no problem. But when the child is asked to think creatively, get something done, show initiative, or follow through on a task, there is a problem.

Many can watch their teacher but when asked to do homework or figure something out that their problems begin. These youngsters think their teacher is there to be absorbed, sort of like they absorb TV.

I know many really creative and productive adults who watch TV mainly when they're too tired to do anything else. TV requires no concentration, no follow-through, no response, no initiative, and no real thought.

It is becoming increasingly clear to us at Evergreen Consultants that the third through sixth years of life are truly critical to the developing brain. It is during these years that initiative and industry should be primary learning goals. These are the years when kids used to make tin can telephones, dress paper dolls, gather the eggs, and learn how to milk the cow.

These are the years that the Flying Wallendas learned how to high-wire walk or that Mozart learned to play and perform on the piano. These are the years when children first spontaneously dance to music, want to help mom clean the kitchen floor, try to help dad with the car, and learn how to put puzzles together.

When children spend thousands of hours in front of the TV—hours during which their brain is developing—they are learning not *to do* but to "be there."

Little kids naturally want to do things with their parents during the critical age from 2 through 6. Parents used to say things like, "Let me help you . . . " or "Why don't you do . . . " Kids had to do something to prevent boredom, even if that meant reading and using their imaginations.

This is no longer true. Many "good" parents have stacks of "good " videos for their children to watch when they get bored. Disney is sold in every grocery store. But as fun as it is to watch, Disney is not nutritious for the developing brain.

We are now convinced that no matter how good the video, on a dynamic level it is really saying, "You don't have to *do* anything to be fascinated." In a Disney movie, the scene may change four times a second. It demands to be experienced, not independently thought about.

And now, all over America, we have a lot of bright little kids running around who are intelligent, who can attend, but who cannot *do* anything without becoming fragmented, hyperactive, or withdrawn.

What to do?

I am reminded of parents who bet their children $100 each that they could not go for one year without TV in the home. These money-hungry kids took their parents on. And they made it for the year.

After collecting their money, the youngsters further shocked their parents by asking that the home continue to be TV-free *without further pay.* They had found a much richer existence, and recognized it for what it was—*doing* things with their parents!

In the next article, Foster explains why the parent-child relationship is so important.

↙୭

A Good Parent/Child Relationship is Essential
Volume 10, no. 2

Everyone knows that it is "nice" for a parent and child to have a close and loving relationship. And almost everyone, on a gut level, feels this is somehow very important. But there are few articles written to help parents understand exactly *why* good parent-child relationships are really so important.

Good parent/child relationships are more than "nice" and "important." Ultimately, they are *essential.* To the extent that a society fosters good parent-child relationships, it will prosper. When, as is the case in modern America, public policy actually encourages poor parent/child relationships, the society will falter and eventually fail.

The formation of conscience

An early good parent-child relationship is essential for conscience formation in a child. All the complex psychic mechanisms that go into the formation of conscience are first built on the infant's and toddler's understanding of, "When Mom is happy, I'm happy; her joy is my joy."

Reciprocal relationships are formed in the very first months of life as an infant smiles at the human face. By six months, an infant has learned that "People are wonderful," or "People cause pain." This early learning is locked in place by the very electro-chemical nature of the brain.

It is very difficult to change these early chemically-set patterns. Trite and simplistic as it may sound, when a little boy cares about his mother, he cares about the world. When he doesn't or can't care about his mom, he doesn't care about anyone else, and his conscience is weak.

Children internalize loving parents

The parent's relationship with the child becomes the basis for all future relationships. Early parent/child relationships are so influential that therapists make big bucks writing books along the lines of *My Mother Myself, How to Get Your Parents Out of Your Head, How to Say No and Not Feel Guilty,* etc.

Thus, the ability to love and maintain close relationships is basically learned from parent/child relationships—not from the first or second spouse. In fact, if the parent/child relationship is rocky, it generally makes for a rocky marital relationship down the road—regardless of the spouse's attempt to change things around.

Effectiveness of isolation as a primary consequence

It is generally believed that God uses isolation as a primary disciplinary technique. Most of the world's great religions, for example, define Hell as separation from God. And most child therapists recommend isolation as a primary consequence. Although there are certainly effective alternatives to the "think-it-over-spot," isolation remains an accepted consequencing technique. It is used when a parent lovingly asks the child to go to his room or otherwise "get lost."

But isolation is only effective when the parent and child have a good relationship. Thus, when a loving parent with a good parent/child relationship says, "Hey, Mark, I'd like you to go somewhere else right now because you're no fun to be around," it means something. Who among us wants to be asked to leave the vicinity of someone we get along with?

But when the relationship is bad, isolation may have no effect whatsoever. Some parents probably unconsciously realize this. But they do things backward by grounding the child to their own vicinity. It's probably true that being forced to be around some parents is punishment enough!

Self-destructive behavior

Good and loving relationships tend to decrease self-destructive behavior in children. Children can be fairly creative in the ways they are self-destructive. Some use suicidal gestures. Others cut school. Some are covertly self-destructive by choosing poor friends or driving carelessly.

Most parents become upset when their children do something that can only end up hurting them. And most parents communicate their feelings, saying in words or actions, "This behavior upsets me," or "This behavior hurts me," or "This behavior makes me really mad."

When a parent communicates pain, hurt, or anger, and the parent/child relationship has turned sour, the child is covertly gratified. Poor parent/child relationships unconsciously produce increased rebellion, acting out and self-destructiveness in general.

Good parent/child relationships are essential if a society or culture is to remain healthy. In the next issue, I will cover the present American government policies that encourage the break-up of the family and make poor parent/child relationships inevitable.

Dysfunctional Families and Government Policy
Volume 10, no. 3

As violent crime and irresponsible behavior continue to increase throughout the country, it's no surprise that our ability, as a population, to accept responsibility for our actions is decreasing.

Easy answers are sought. TV violence has been blamed, as has the availability of handguns. The problem with the latter explanation, of course, is the fact that handguns have always been available. Those states and districts with the strictest handgun laws still have high crime rates.

Regarding TV violence, there are few shows as violent as the fairy tales many of us grew up with. Obviously, Little Red Riding Hood's grandmother being eaten by a wolf, who in turn is axed to death by a huntsman, would be considered violent by today's standards.

Unfortunately, the real cause of violence comes from the way many infants and toddlers are treated today. America is getting what America deserves.

Americans have elected officials who promote irresponsible behavior in both our ability to work and to parent. Citizens who are either unwilling or unable to hold a job for even six months are encouraged by the government to have children. They are paid, per baby, to produce children who are often abused, neglected, and ultimately turned over to the welfare system.

These unfortunate and ruined children, many who grow up to be violent, are paid and cared for by responsible young citizens who cannot afford children of their own because they're too busy paying taxes to support other people's children.

Thus, in America, there are literally millions of people who can't parent and can't hold jobs who are home raising irresponsible children. And there are millions of responsible working women who would make good mothers, but are unable to afford staying home with their children. In essence, they are forced to pay for the ruination of children produced by others.

The Hostile-dependent cycle

It is both enlightening and necessary to examine government policies and contrast them with healthy family functioning. The destructiveness of government policies then becomes very apparent.

Sadly, things that would be considered "sick" in a family are now standard government procedure. In many cities, for instance, government authorities advocate providing addicts with clean needles. However, a therapist would regard it as a sign of sickness for the mother of a 30-year-old to note in therapy: "I'm so concerned about George. He's on drugs and I know that it's illegal, but I'm worried about him being infected with dirty needles. So dad and I have the kettle boiling in the kitchen all the time to sterilize his needles . . . "

"Hostile-dependent" is an old psychological term that is relevant today. It describes the behavior of children whose parents overprotect or give to them regardless of whether they do anything for themselves. As the giving continues, the child comes to depend increasingly on the giving. Predictable escalation to a tragic, inevitable outcome inevitably occurs.

The cycle of hostile-dependency is as follows: The child has an increasingly poor self-image while becoming increasingly demanding of the parents—who now start feeling resentful but continue to "give all we can." Finally, the parents reach their breaking point at which they can no longer give. The child goes into a rage of resentment and entitlement. Not infrequently the child kills the parents.

Large segments of the American population, perhaps even large segments of the world, are now hostile-dependent. Legislation has mandated that individuals remain fragmented and dependent to receive government help. A recent article commented on this:

> Millions of inner-city dwellers "choose" single motherhood only because government makes it look like a good deal. Government offers the unmarried mother an attractive contractual arrangement: the equivalent of somewhere between $8,500 and $15,000 per year in combined welfare benefits on the condition that the young woman not work for pay, and not marry an employed male.

> What the government offers her is a classic contract. In consideration of the government's offer of a package of benefits, the mother agrees not to engage in the activities that are crucial to the formation of a decent society. Government has bargained for social breakdown, and it has gotten it. (Gary Bauer, *Washington Watch*, Vol. 3 (9), June 1992.)

Truly, what healthy parent would say this to his own children, "Honey, have as many children as you want. I'll pay the obstetrical costs for all of them. I'll pay all the childcare costs that I can. I'll help you with rent and food as much as I can. And, I'll even pay the funeral costs for you and your children. However, promise me that you won't marry anyone who is capable of helping with these expenses."

What parent would respond by giving money every month to a daughter or son who stopped by to say, "You know, Dad, it's so hard to make ends meet when Fran and I are both on drugs. We just can't hold regular jobs, and you know the drugs are so expensive anyhow. So I'm just dropping by for my monthly food and rent check. Bye."

In Hennipen County, Minnesota, it is estimated the average welfare mother receives $20,000 per year in the combined benefits of welfare, housing subsidies, and food stamps. It would be economic suicide to give up these benefits when the government requires *leisure* and the option is *work!*

It must be remembered that the $20,000 being paid to the welfare recipient is nearly matched dollar for dollar by the salaries of government employees who dole out the money. Presently, nearly half of all Americans work, in one way or another, for a government agency.

The government's unspoken assumption is that *poverty, rather than the destruction of the family,* is the determining factor in raising healthy, rather than emotionally sick, children. Actually, it is the other way around. Study after study shows that poverty, in and of itself, has nothing to do with child-rearing. All over the world, working, poverty-stricken families do a wonderful job of raising their children.

A recent study demonstrated that poverty was not the key factor, *even with single urban mothers.* (C. Rodning, L. Beckwith and J. Howard, "Quality of attachment and home environments in children prenatally exposed to PCP and cocaine," *Development and Psychopathology* 3 (1991), pp. 351-356.)

The problem of finding people who want to work is understandable. One of my secretaries, while typing this manuscript, noted, "Gee, Foster, what am I working for? A welfare mother doing nothing makes more than I make working part-time for you."

That governmental programs foster hostile-dependent behavior was recently brought home to me. A school psychologist, who I considered to be bright, motivated and responsible, recently had experienced a cut in her program. She, along with others, was let go by the county school system.

She called me to consult on a case, as she was seeing private clients on the side. Before hanging up, almost parenthetically, she said, "As you know, I've been dropped by the system. Actually, I'm enjoying my vacation. It's great to be paid not to go to work every day. But Foster, to qualify for unemployment, I have to make two contacts a week for a job. Can I use this phone call as one of my contacts? *Isn't the government dumb?"* Even she was driven to bite the hand that was unwisely feeding her.

Society, like some parents, appears to have great difficulty separating the "can'ts" from the "won'ts." If a person—of any age—is treated as "unable," that individual becomes increasingly debilitated.

Every parent has had the experience of dealing with a child who doesn't do her chores. Is it a question of the child not wanting to empty the trash or of the child being "unable" to empty the trash?

When parents define the problem as a disability, what may originally have been an attitude problem becomes an angry demand for assistance: "You need to help me, Mom!"

Our government is unwisely responding to the same cry from too many of its citizens.

Foster's next article shows parents how to quash biting behavior.

Children Who Bite
Volume 10, no. 4

One could speculate on the reasons children bit each other or their parents: We might speculate that children, like all humans, are simply meat eaters. But there is probably a better way to understand biting.

Or, we could speculate that they have a need to teethe on something and a sibling or parent is the closest thing at hand—but there has to be a better way to understand biting.

Perhaps, as Freud said, children go through an "oral aggressive" period. That is, he found, children naturally and normally may express their angry and aggressive feelings by chomping on someone or something in the environment. This is undoubtedly true. Biting, then, is a phase. It will pass, and if nothing at all were done about it, most adults never would express their anger by chewing on someone else.

The question is: Can we help speed children through this phase? Happily, the answer is yes!

How to handle biting

First, the child must get the message that biting is absolutely, without a doubt, unacceptable behavior. Most of you will say, "Well of course it is unacceptable! Why would Foster be telling us that?"

Actually, down deep inside, parents may not regard biting as absolutely unacceptable. In my years as a child psychiatrist, I have seen more than a few misguided parents, after a bite, exclaim to their child, "Oh, wow! Why would you do that to Mommy?" It is as if they expect their child to say, "One, I hate you; two, I am hungry; three, you overreact"; etc.

Most importantly, the correct response to biting must be based on the bact that all children love to force an emotional response from a parent and hate being consequenced in a matter-of-fact way. Biting is often unwittingly reinforced by parents who overreact when their child suddenly bites. And it is easy to get loud and angry about that.

From the child's point of view, it is fun to see someone you love get that noisy. It's a lot more exciting to get a parent to light up and go off than it is to light a sparkler on the Fourth of July. If the parent and child have a conflicted or angry relationship, it is particularly gratifying for the child if the parent will become noisy, because the child consciously or unconsciously actually wants to upset the parent.

So when the parent/child relationship is good, it is fun and exciting when parents get noisy and put out, but if the relationship is bad, then it is doubly outright wonderful!

So handling biting correctly, like handling pooping in the pants, hair-pulling, and biting the fingernails, must be carried out quietly and effectively rather than noisily and ineffectively.

The natural response to any overt aggression is to respond in kind. And I have to be honest and state that many parents have reported this to be an effective response.

But to be effective, it must be done without overt anger and should be carried out playfully, but with vigor: "I bet my hand tasted good to you! Like strawberry! Shall we keep tasting each other? No? Well, OK, Sweetie, but it is fun at times to taste the other guy. Any time you want to have a 'taste each other party,' give me a bite. You don't want to? Well, OK . . . "

Jesus had to plead with people to turn the other cheek, because turning the other cheek is not very natural. Turning the other cheek may work well over time with adults who have an available conscience. They are expected to come around to the conclusion: "Geez, I keep biting this person, and they love me anyway; perhaps I should change my behavior and back off."

This change in behavior, however, does not come immediately. One might say it was too slow for Jesus himself! Saying, in essence, "Bite on, I know you'll outgrow it," may be developmentally correct, but by then a sibling could be fairly well chewed up.

The officially recommended response to biting is to *firmly, quietly and quickly* isolate the child from others immediately after the child has nibbled on someone else. This is usually effective. The older the child, the longer the child needs to be isolated.

Isolation generally has to be much more than "one minute per year of age." I don't know who thought up this often quoted formula, but isolating a child one minute per year of age is akin to sending serial killer to jail for a month for every year of age. It just isn't long enough! Usually the isolation needs to be at least 15 minutes for a 2- or 3-year-old, and longer for older children.

In addition, the child needs to be encouraged when he or she has played for a time without biting. This is the "catch 'em in the microsecond that they're good" routine: "Oh, I like seeing you play so happily with Susan. That makes me happy, too."

There must be encouragement for the correct behavior and quiet, quick, and consistent consequences for the bad behavior. When the child handles the situation correctly, *then* get noisy and congratulate. *Do something and be quiet* when the behavior is bad.

The Authors

Jim Fay, with over 30 years experience in education, is nationally recognized as a consultant in behavior management and is one of America's most sought-after presenters on parenting and school discipline. Jim teaches seminars and workshops for parents and educators throughout the United States, Canada, and Europe, and is the author of over 90 books, audios, and articles on parenting and positive discipline. His humorous style and charisma have made him a favorite personality on hundreds of radio and television talk shows.

Foster W. Cline, M.D. is an internationally-acclaimed adult and child psychiatrist, author, consultant, and speaker. He is recognized for his theories of child development and has received wide acclaim for his effective treatment of severely emotionally disturbed children. Foster is known for helping parents and children with practical techniques that have immediate results. His delightful speaking style has been enjoyed by parents, educators, and therapists throughout the world.

Jim and Foster's "Love and Logic" philosophy has revolutionized the way parents, teachers and professionals work with children. Jim and Foster are the co-founders of the Love and Logic Institute, Inc. of Golden, Colorado, which carries an extensive line of Love and Logic support materials.

For information on any of the materials mentioned in the text or for a free catalog of Love and Logic CD's, DVD's, books and training curricula, please visit our web-site at www.loveandlogic.com or call us toll free at 1-800-338-4065.